*"In the minds of great managers [manacoaches], consistent poor performance is not primarily a matter of weakness, stupidity, disobedience, or disrespect. It is a matter of miscasting."*

—**Marcus Buckingham**, Author of *First Break All The Rules*

*"Most business owners need to understand that although they might be great leaders, they might not be great managers. Understanding the distinction made clear in this book could definitely help you to* Finish Big.

—**Bo Burlingham**, Author of *Finish Big, Small Giants,* and *The Great Game of Business,* and Editor at large at Inc. Magazine

*"I'm fortunate to spend more than a hundred days each year working with the leadership teams of entrepreneurial companies. If you read nothing else in Kevin's book, pay attention to the chapter on vulnerability. In my experience, it's impossible to be an effective manager if you aren't willing and able to be transparent and real."*

—**Mike Paton**, Visionary, EOS Worldwide, and best-selling Author of *Get A Grip: How to Get Everything You Want from Your Entrepreneurial Business*

*"Read this book if you want to know why leaders can make lousy managers. I discovered the difference, and it has made an impact on the bottom lines of my clients."*

—**Ruth King** , Profitability Master and Author of the #1 bestselling book, *The Courage to be Profitable*

"Finally, a book that clarified exactly the difference between 'Leadership' and 'Management.' Kevin has been able to articulate the differences when others such as Jim Collins and Pat Lencioni who are icons in the field use them as if they were interchangeable. Love it!"

—**Gregory Cleary**, Founder, Pinnacle Business Guides

"From this book, I realized that I want to be a leader, but when you have people working for you, you need to be a good manager. I reference the book a lot. It is a great management textbook for me. I love how Kevin wrote it, and it taught me a lot about how to manage people to be curious, make solid business decisions, and make a difference in moving the company forward."

—**Susan O'Kelley**, CFO, PCE Pacific, Inc.

"Kevin's insights on leadership have always been on target and more importantly have proven extremely valuable in my development as a leader and have been a key driver of Unitech's incredible success."

—**Rick Boates**, President, Unitech Construction Management

"This book caused me to rethink some of my long-chariest beliefs. It not only serves as a primer for the uninitiated in this field but as a challenging catalyst for retrospection for the serious student of management and leadership. It should be a mandatory read for those who find themselves leading a cause or managing others."

—**Perry Niehaus**, President and CEO, Laservalley Technologies

"*Reinforced by solid research data and real-life experiences, Kevin has delivered a clear and concise guideline for anyone who is or wants to be a manacoach. If it weren't for the people, business would be easy. Discover in this great read the tools that make the people element of business a whole lot easier. Keep it on hand at the office. If you are a business leader, read this book! And ensure your manacoach reads this book. If you are a manacoach, read this book and flourish as a successful manacoach who is getting things done efficiently and effectively through other people.*"

—**Doug Friesen**, President and CEO, TAK Logistics

"*This book is chock-full of wisdom for those who actually manage today's successful businesses. It takes a deep dive into the role of world class, key managers and the critical role they play in winning organizations. Read* The Miracle Manager *today. You'll be richer for it.*"

—**Bill Seelig**, EOS Implementer, TAB Franchisee, Seelig & Company

"*Small business owners! Leaders are not Managers! And they don't need to be. I was expecting another book on managing that walked me through steps of how to manage my employees. Instead, I got pretty much hit between the eyeballs of some amazing insights from Armstrong. I hope you find the read as refreshing and energizing as I did.*"

—**Amazon.com Customer Review**

*"The best part of this book is the simple, powerful context that leaders just lead. This is exactly why management (or, manacoaches,) are a necessity. Great work Kevin!"*

**—Preston True,** Founding Member, Pinnacle Business Guides; Founder, Get TPA Fit

*"I have had the pleasure of hearing Kevin speak and highly recommend his book. He points out the waste of good leaders and managers being placed in roles not meant for them that constantly leads to human capital waste in business. A must read by a passionate and compassionate author."*

**—Al Zdenek,** Author of *Master Your Business Cash Flow*, Speaker, Wealth Advisor

*"A fantastic read if you want to be able to quickly identify what skills you have as a manager and what skills you may need to develop. Armstrong shows good examples, as well as stories of the need to be honest with who you are and accountable to what you can bring to the table. And then an organization can truly thrive."*

**—Dave Shaw**, Managing Partner, Island Glass & Mirror Ltd.

*"If you are ready to get past your ego and realize your, and your organization's potential, read this book! I wish I had learned these concepts earlier on in my career!"*

**—Rachel Wolfe**, MBA, Business Advisor & Chief Integration Officer, The Interdependent Training Group Inc.

*"My MBA degree did not teach me what Kevin Armstrong has to say in this book."*

**—Bruce Der**, P. ENG., MBA, President and CEO, A.H. Lundberg Systems

# THE MIRACLE MANAGER

*Why true leaders*
*rarely make*
*great managers*

## KEVIN G. ARMSTRONG

**Forbes**Books

Published by ForbesBooks, Charleston, South Carolina.
Member of Advantage Media Group.

ForbesBooks is a registered trademark, and the ForbesBooks colophon is a trademark of Forbes Media, LLC.

Printed in the United States of America.

10 9 8 7 6 5 4 3

ISBN: 978-1-946633-00-2
LCCN: 2017934106

Cover design by George Stevens.

This publication is designed to provide accurate and authoritative information in regard to the subject matter covered. It is sold with the understanding that the publisher is not engaged in rendering legal, accounting, or other professional services. If legal advice or other expert assistance is required, the services of a competent professional person should be sought.

Advantage Media Group is proud to be a part of the Tree Neutral® program. Tree Neutral offsets the number of trees consumed in the production and printing of this book by taking proactive steps such as planting trees in direct proportion to the number of trees used to print books. To learn more about Tree Neutral, please visit **www.treeneutral.com.**

Since 1917, the Forbes mission has remained constant. Global Champions of Entrepreneurial Capitalism. ForbesBooks exists to further that aim by bringing the Stories, Passion, and Knowledge of top thought leaders to the forefront. ForbesBooks brings you The Best in Business. To be considered for publication, please visit **www.forbesbooks.com**

# Contents

## CHAPTER 1
## MY PROMISE TO YOU . . . . . . . . . . . . . . . . . . . . . 1

We Can All Relate

A Long History of Confusing Two Roles

My Promise

## CHAPTER 2
## A LEADER STANDS ALONE . . . . . . . . . . . . . . . . . . . 9

Is a True Leader Concerned with Who Is Following?

Failure Is a Prerequisite

Leading, Not Managing

## CHAPTER 3
## THE MANACOACH . . . . . . . . . . . . . . . . . . . . . . . 19

The Manacoach Defined

The Manacoach Test

Understanding Your Results

Differences Explained

An Example of a Leader versus a Manacoach

## CHAPTER 4
## DOES A STAR MAKE A GOOD MANAGER? ........ 39

Who Is a Better Coach?

Running the Numbers on Players and Coaches

Ice Hockey

Basketball

Baseball

Why Doesn't Business Reward the Players?

## CHAPTER 5
## CULTURE AND THE MANACOACH .............. 51

What Is Culture?

Status over Achievement

Are You Trapped as a Manacoach?

What Do I Look for When I'm Hiring?

## CHAPTER 6
## THERE IS NO POWER WITHOUT VULNERABILITY ... 63

Depth

Why Vulnerability Is Hard Work

Finding Our Vulnerabilities

If You Can't Be Vulnerable, Don't Manage People

# CHAPTER 7
## THE MANACOACH ON HIRING . . . . . . . . . . . . . . . . . . 77

The Ideal Candidate

Measuring the Alignment of Core Values

Linking the Right Person to the Right Job

Reference Checks

Behavior Assessments

Giving the Green Light to Proceed

# CHAPTER 8
## THE MANACOACH ON FIRING . . . . . . . . . . . . . . . . . . 91

Attitude/Values

Performance

Ability to Complete

# CHAPTER 9
## DELEGATING AND DEPENDENCE . . . . . . . . . . . . . . . 111

Dependence: You Get What You Put Up With!

Insecurities with Delegating

Not Knowing How to Delegate

Not Wanting to Go Home

Rejecting the Dependence

## CHAPTER 10
## COMMUNICATION . . . . . . . . . . . . . . . . . . . . . . . . . . . 127

Quit Hiding behind Your Keyboard!

Dare to Enter the Danger

Interpretation

Politics versus Accountability

## CHAPTER 11
## REWARDS AND PUNISHMENTS . . . . . . . . . . . . . . . . 139

Why Bonuses and Profit Sharing
Don't Work in Most Cases

The Carrot and Stick Method Doesn't Work

## CHAPTER 12
## BE BOLD AND BE S.M.A.R.T. . . . . . . . . . . . . . . . . . 147

Be S.M.A.R.T.

What Are the Conditions?

## CONCLUDING REMARKS . . . . . . . . . . . . . . . . . . . . . 153

My Type of Leader

Final Thoughts on the Manacoach

## APPENDIX
## THE MANACOACH'S CHECKLIST . . . . . . . . . . . . . . . 159

*chapter 1*

# MY PROMISE TO YOU

*"There are leaders and there are those who lead. Leaders hold a position of power, or authority, but those who lead, inspire us . . . we follow those who lead not because we have to but because we want to. We follow those who lead not for them but for ourselves."*

**—SIMON SINEK**

It all started many years ago . . .

I was hired as a vice president for a fairly large financial company. While I was still learning what I should do in the role, I went for dinner with a colleague who was the VP of the finance department. While we were eating, he informed me that I had to learn how to become a good manager. I asked him for his definition of one, but he couldn't produce an answer that made sense. Since then, for over three decades, I have contemplated my own answers to that question. You might say it's become an obsession.

I'm writing this book because we are losing sight of the crucial difference between leadership and management. A leader is not concerned about influencing others and may not possess top-notch communication skills, charisma, or even a likable personality. Leadership does not depend on how you look or how you come across or even how well you speak in public. A manager, though, needs all of these.

This book focuses on making you a better manager. However, in order to do that, we must clearly understand—and I mean *crystal clear*—what management is. Great managers know how to identify great leaders and their shining ideas. Yet a leader needs only to march forward. A manager has to marshal all of the troops and make sure everyone is marching in the same direction. A manager must have integrity, which is best defined as consistency between what you think, say, and do. And integrity is measured only on what you do—not what you say.

I decided to title this book *The Miracle Manager* because I was so impressed with the movie *Miracle*. Kurt Russell played the role of Herb Brooks, an extraordinary coach who took the US Olympic hockey team to a gold medal in 1980. Herb Brooks did not make the Olympic team as a player, back in the 1960s. He was cut. But although he wasn't a great player, an Internet search of the all-time top coaches will turn up the name Herb Brooks. He wasn't necessarily a leader on skates, but he was a leading-edge coach on the bench.

## We Can All Relate

Have you ever worked for a bad manager—someone who took all the credit when things were good and laid all the blame on others when things went wrong? Someone who didn't know how to teach and just expected you to know things? Someone who was only interested in his own status and well-being? Someone who was only interested in her own survival? If you are answering yes to each of these questions, consider yourself in the norm.

Now let's move on to the next questions. How did the experience of being managed like that make you feel? Did you feel like you wanted to do a better job? Did you feel understood, valued, and inspired to be a better person? Did you feel like you were on a great team or part of a healthy culture? Did you feel like you wanted to bring 110 percent of your knowledge, talent, and potential to work every day? Did you feel like someone was watching your back no matter what went down?

If your answer is no to these questions, you are, unfortunately, among the many and not the few. Everyone has had a bad manager. Many of us have never had a great manager.

## A Long History of Confusing Two Roles

This is a book written for the people who know that enhancing managers and management techniques is the only real way to create healthier and more productive organizational cultures. It's for those who recognize that respectable team members will trade wages and even benefits to work in a healthy organizational culture . . . and more importantly, they will work hard! This book is for you if you want to become a better manager by understanding the significant difference between exceptional management and great leadership. Perhaps you are just entering the management ranks. Perhaps you are an active business owner who realizes that you aren't a good manager. Or perhaps you are a good manager who wants to become better (my favorite type). If you fall into one, or all, of these categories, this book will be valuable.

The first thing you must understand is that this book is not about leadership. This central principle is a bold new departure from other books written on management. In order to better define what makes a manager exceptional, we need to examine the differences between leadership and management. We have to quit using them as synonyms. Empirical data shows that many businesses make a significant mistake when they allow, entice, persuade, bribe, or outright force their leaders into positions of management, because this frequently results in those leaders failing. Leaders shifted into management based solely on their ability to lead have only a one in five, or 20 percent, chance at succeeding in this new role. Yet businesses continue to make this tempting mistake all the time.

Tom Peters, author of the bestseller *In Search of Excellence* and a respected speaker and business nut that myself and thousands of others have followed for over three decades, says in a YouTube video in a frustrated and depressed voice, "Only in the stupid world of business and government do we promote the best accountant to the head of the accounting department, the best salesman to the head of the sales department, the best trainer to the head of the training department. We don't do that in sports, right? The definition of most of our coaches at the professional level is they were second rate or marginal players who were brilliant students at the game and 'people'." This book will support this statement more than you know, but even Tom at times uses the word "leader" inappropriately.

The confusion between the terms "leader" and "manager" exists for a very good reason. Some of the most respected business schools, authors, and researchers constantly interchange the terms. Here are some examples.

Patrick Lencioni has written some amazing business fables over the years. I have worked face-to-face with more than two hundred business owners from every type of industry, and every time Lencioni publishes a fable, I give a copy to my clients as a gift. The principles he has shared in his books have been shared in my seminars for years now. I have seen amazing results and transitions come from his ideas. However, as much as I respect the man as a management/people guru, he confuses his audience by flipping back and forth between the terms "management" and "leadership."

Here is a quote from his book *The Advantage*:

> It's also critical for *leaders* to realize that no upward communications program will ever take the place of a *manager* who understands and represents the views of his or her employees. One of the most common complaints of unhealthy organizations has to do with breakdowns in communication across departments or divisions. And as much as *leaders* might want to implement special communication programs to alleviate this, the only good way to address it is to attack the root cause: unresolved issues among the *leaders* of those divisions. (italics added)

When Patrick uses the word "manager," is he referring to a "manager" or a "leader"? What is he referring to in the last sentence when he uses the word "leader"? Patrick also uses the word "executive" throughout his writings, and it's difficult to know whether this term is referring to a leader or a manager, which only adds to the confusion.

Jim Collins has earned widespread respect with his research and writing in books like *Built to Last*, *Good to Great*, and *Great by Choice*. His "20 Mile March" concept, explained in *Great by Choice*, is nothing short of genius. However, the qualities of the "Level 5 Leaders" in *Good to Great* mostly concern "Level 5 Managers"—not leaders. He too confuses his audiences by using these two words as synonyms.

Tom Peters points out in the same YouTube presentation mentioned previously that he taught Jim Collins when they were both at Stanford University. Peters doesn't agree with a single word that Collins has written on "leadership." I don't either unless, when

Collins writes "leader" or "leadership," you replace it with "manager" and "management." Then everything Collins finds in his research makes more sense.

Here is my all-time favorite example: Liz Wiseman and Greg McKeown wrote a masterpiece, *Multipliers: How the Best Leaders Make Everyone Smarter*, on what makes great managers. Yet here is a quote from an article in the *Harvard Business Review* written by Greg McKeown: "After studying 150 *leaders* in 35 companies across 4 continents, our research suggests that most *managers* under-estimate how widely employees' talent is under-utilized." (italics added)

The very title of Wiseman and McKeown's book is confusing: do "leaders" make everyone smarter or do "multipliers"? Even the late, great Stephen Covey acknowledged the book, but he confuses us when introducing the book by saying, "a great insight is that 'multipliers' are hard edged managers. There is nothing soft about these 'leaders.'"

Are multipliers great leaders or managers? Wiseman and McKeown make statements in the book like: "Vikram worked as a *manager* under two different division managers at Intel. Each *leader* could be considered a genius," or "the second *manager* was brilliant, who had now been promoted into management to run the plant… the problem was that this *leader* did all the thinking." (italics added)

Peter Drucker is considered by many to be a management "guru," yet it was his position that there was no difference between a leader and a manager.

Like so many other authors, Wiseman, McKeown, and Peter Drucker use the words *leader*, *manager*, and *executive* like they are synonyms.

McKeown's book *Essentialism* is brilliant and an essential read for managers and leaders alike. I recommend it to every manager

I speak to. But here too, he uses the two words as synonyms through-out his book.

After reading this book, you will be convinced that using these words indiscriminately is at best creating confusion and at worst causing havoc in business. Once at a seminar, a colleague stood up and said, "You can't be a great leader without having a great team." The whole audience, excluding myself, nodded their heads in agreement. The same thing happened at another conference where an attendee stood up and said, "You aren't a true leader unless you have produced another leader." Although these statements may sound profound, do they really make any sense?

## My Promise

Since the turn of the century, I have taught and stand behind the works and findings of all of these great authors. I call the great manager a "manacoach," and Wiseman and McKeown use the term "multi-plier." You are flat-out crazy *not* to read Wiseman and McKeown's book, because it will make you a better manacoach if you have the talent for that role. Patrick Lencioni's *The Five Temptations of a CEO* is a bible for managers who want to improve their skills and abilities. If you want to be a better businessperson or manager, you would be well advised to read everything Jim Collins has ever published.

But the question is, are managers and leaders the same? Marcus Buckingham, coauthor of *First Break All the Rules* with Curt Coffman, has written a bible for the manacoach in any organization. Bucking-ham bases a lot of findings from years of working with data from the Gallup Organization, and like me, he states that there is a very significant difference between a manager and a leader.

By the end of this book, I promise that you will know the differ-ence between a manager and a leader. When that is understood, you will know what it takes to be an effective manager (a manacoach). I assure you that this book will be short and easy to understand. The findings and principles will be simple and backed by solid data and experience—not theory. But make no mistake: rarely does *simple* mean *easy*. In fact, after reading this book, you might decide that management is not for you. In reality, it's definitely not for everyone and very few are good at it.

In almost every performance activity in our society besides business, we rightfully give far more recognition and rewards to leaders than we do to managers. One of our root assumptions is that, like sports, business is a performance activity. That's why this book looks at different sports stars and explains why they didn't become good managers. You will learn why a company's culture is so important to how a manacoach directs a team. This book also explores the powerful concept that you cannot have power without being willing to be vulnerable. Such training will guide how you make the decisions to hire new employees and fire nonperformers. Other chapters in this book will show the necessity of learning how to delegate the workload. That is part and parcel of the crucial managerial skill of *communication*. When you have mastered that art, you will be able to issue rewards and punishments for reasons that everyone can understand.

I am so confident that this book will help you identify what a good manager should be and apply those lessons to your current business techniques that if for some reason it doesn't, I will give you a full refund for this book. That is a personal guarantee.

*chapter 2*

# A LEADER STANDS ALONE

*"A genuine leader is not a searcher for consensus but a molder of consensus."*

## —MARTIN LUTHER KING JR.

Bill is what I like to call a "disruptor." Although the term is usually regarded as negative, disruptors are very much an active part of healthy organizations. Bill goes to a seminar with five hundred others to listen to a self-professed expert on the concept of leadership. This expert is Dr. Jones, who talks about how leaders influence people to learn and grow. Dr. Jones goes on to talk about how leaders give clear direction, deal with people effectively, and motivate people. Dr. Jones has a PhD in leadership and an MBA from a prestigious university, not to mention two best sellers he has written on the topic of leadership.

As a natural disruptor—a personality trait found in many leaders—Bill is one of those guys sitting in the audience who is not afraid to raise his hand when things don't make sense. He doesn't care how many people are in the room. So in front of five hundred people, even though Dr. Jones said at the beginning of the presentation to hold questions until the end, Bill shoots his hand in the air.

Of course, our disruptor is always sitting at the front of the room, right in front of the speaker, so Dr. Jones can't finish his presentation without acknowledging Bill. He points to Bill and asks if he has a question.

Bill thanks Dr. Jones and proceeds to walk up to the microphone on the floor because he wants everyone to hear his question.

"A twenty-two-year old male is up at a ski resort. He's going back to his hotel at two o'clock after a night at the bar, and he cuts through the parking lot to shorten the walk. In the middle of the night, with nobody else to see or be seen, the young man sees that a garbage container, which should be secured, is actually unlocked and tipped over, with garbage scattered over the ground.

"The young man knows that this is potentially a bad situation. It is dangerous for bears because if they become used to eating food provided by humans, they will have to be put down. Also, because bears are wild and therefore unpredictable, it's unsafe for the community if the bears hang around, as some innocent person could be attacked for no apparent reason. So without hesitation, this young man walks over, cleans up the smelly trash, puts it back in the container, and secures it. There is not one person in the vicinity. Visibility is poor due to snow falling, and it's pitch dark out. So I need to ask you, Dr. Jones, even though there was nobody to lead, nobody to influence, and nobody to hold accountable, would what this young man did be considered leadership?"

Dr. Jones doesn't think very hard before responding. "No, that is not considered leadership. That's considered a good deed."

Bill doesn't agree. People from the audience start to chime in that they agree with Bill the disruptor.

## Is a True Leader Concerned with Who Is Following?

What do you think? We are taught that the point of leadership is leading people, but there was nobody to lead in the scenario with the parking lot trash can.

Stephen Covey once said, "Leadership is *doing the right thing*, and management is *doing things right*." (italics added) If that is the case, both Bill and the young man securing the garbage from the bears are leaders. Their ability to take a stand is similar to when Gandhi started his movement for peaceful resistance. Most great leaders act alone because they stick with their own intentions, which are based on their core values. True leaders don't care whether or not anyone is following them.

To show why this is true, it makes sense to draw a comparison to political leaders. What do Rosa Parks, Martin Luther King Jr., Mahatma Gandhi, and Nelson Mandela have in common? They all broke laws set by their society, they all spent time in jail, and yet their names are always found in lists of the top fifty leaders of all time. This clearly shows that a leader's thoughts can be so disruptive that people aren't ready for them.

Most of the books on the subject tell you that leaders are always looking to the future, always looking for a better alternative. What they believe, what they say, and what they do are always consistent. This is the definition of "integrity," which is only measured on your actions. As Robert Fulghum says in his book *All I Really Need to Know I Learned in Kindergarten*: "Don't be concerned that your children don't listen to you; be more concerned that they are watching you."

People crave integrity. It is a staple ingredient of trust. We are inspired by the person who acts on a belief of what is truly right or is necessary to make something better. As a person with integrity starts down a path, we may follow, not because of that person, but because of what he or she believes to be right. Simon Sinek points out that leaders make us feel safe.

Simon also points out another key component of leadership. Martin Luther King Jr. didn't compromise his beliefs. He didn't present a plan. He shared what he believed, and whether people followed or not, he wasn't going to change that belief.

Let's take a look at a different type of leadership, from the ground up. When Rosa Parks took that seat in the front of a Montgomery, Alabama, bus—where only whites could legally sit—she was breaking the law, and she knew it. She was a true leader, and yet it's safe to say that she wasn't thinking about influencing or persuading people to do something. She wasn't thinking about holding people accountable. She wasn't thinking about how to make people feel "empowered" or "motivated." She had decided that enough was enough and the law was simply wrong. Regardless of what anyone else said, Parks wasn't moving. She had arrived at a point where she was going to face the consequences of her actions because sitting in the back of the bus didn't make sense to her.

However, in contrast to leaders like Richard Nixon and others who feel that they are bigger than the law, the critical difference is that Parks wasn't breaking the law to protect herself or to gain anything of material value. She was breaking a law that in her mind was unjust. She made the decision of a person who acts in accordance with what she believes, no matter what anyone else thinks. Her decision was that of a great leader.

The same principle holds true in the world of business. I have been working with the owners of small and mid-sized businesses for over two decades, and with the rare exception, most of them eventually run into trouble because of the very leadership skills that got them started. That includes the plumber who started a plumbing business, the electrician who started an electrical business, the computer expert who started a computer service company, and the lawyer who started a law firm. They had all of the skills of a leader. They had vision, in that they could see a need for what they offered. They had the courage to go out on their own and do what they thought was the right thing to do.

Sometimes that strategy really pays off. Take the example of Rick Boates, who owns Unitech Construction Management. Unitech recommends the best strategies and the best providers of services, and they provide total transparency in what is being charged and what Unitech is making. A typical contractor guarantees a price and then works with their subcontractors to complete the project. You have no idea what the contractor is making on the job. Unitech constructs a lot of government projects like schools, municipal recreations centers, and port terminals. A few years ago, the government where Unitech does business decided to invite only "design/build" companies to propose bids. Without going into detail, this policy change meant that Unitech didn't have a chance at getting any of the jobs unless they were willing to change their model.

I worked closely with Rick while his banks, his partners, his employees, and his board relentlessly pressured him to change his business model and conform to the design/build model. Rick didn't care about what anyone else thought. Unitech had built its reputation on providing construction management services, and he wasn't going to change. The government and large businesses eventually learned that design/build wasn't all it was cracked up to be, and today Unitech is having the best run in its thirty-year history.

Bruce Der made a different type of business decision, but his leadership was crucial all the same. Bruce is president of A.H. Lundberg Systems. The company has been around for over fifty years, and up until a few years ago, they provided design and equipment engineering services to the pulp industry. That's when Bruce realized that pulp production was moving from North America to Asia. He knew that his business would shrink if he didn't find other markets to service, so Lundberg Systems (under Bruce's direction) made a strategic move to shift to the oil and gas industry. Bruce realized that the same types of devices they engineered to make pulp and paper mills more environmentally friendly could be easily adapted for the oil and gas industry. As a leader, Bruce looked into the future and made tough decisions.

Rick and Bruce didn't care about what was safe or easy. When you run a business where your employees and their families, your suppliers, your customers, and your own family rely on your decisions as a leader, you and you alone have to make the tough decisions.

It's interesting to note that as great leaders, both Rick and Bruce hire great managers.

Rick, Bruce, and the hundreds of other business owners I have had the privilege of working with over the years are just like the young man who cleans up the garbage because it's the right thing to do. They look into the future with the information they have at hand, and they make a decision. If it turns out to be an unpopular one, they don't care what anyone else thinks. They don't care who was behind them or beside them. They did what, in their hearts, was the right thing to do.

## Failure Is a Prerequisite

You need leaders on the team to succeed. They climb the tree to see if things are moving in the right direction. They know where "true north" is at all times. Leaders are not afraid to experiment with new and more efficient ways to do things. They are constantly taking risks, even if they make no sense to anyone but themselves, because they know that failure is a mandatory part of success. A true leader's motto is, "The biggest risk in life is taking no risk at all." They have self-confidence in their choices, and at times a high ego, especially in their area of expertise.

Formal education is not a requirement or even a common trait among the world's top leaders. Bill Gates, Steve Jobs, Henry Ford, Ray Kroc, Walt Disney, and many others had natural leadership skills that cemented their permanent place in history, but many of them, including the ones just named, dropped out of school at various levels. In sales, you have to fail to succeed . . . you have to thrive on rejection. From my observations, the more institutional education we have, the more we are taught that failure is to be avoided at all costs.

I will never forget the inspirational words painted on the wall at a pool where I swam laps: "It's not over when you fail, it's over when you quit." That is the motto of a true leader, yet many of our institutions and formal training programs teach that if you fail at a task or test, you are a "failure" and should quit. If you want to learn more about the failure of our school system in nurturing and developing true leaders, study the works of Sir Ken Robinson or watch his presentations on TED.com. One of his best insights is, "We stigmatize mistakes. And we're now running national educational systems where mistakes are the worst thing you can make—and the result is that we are educating people out of their creative capacities. . . . Sometimes getting away from school is the best thing that can happen to a great mind."

Over the years we have studied great salespeople to see what traits they share, if any. Although we don't have the data to back this finding, one of the things we discovered is that great salespeople usually have little or no postsecondary education. I've concluded that this is because the education system teaches us to avoid failure and that failure is wrong. Because you might have to get five noes before you get a yes, failure is a critical component of success in sales.

## Leading, Not Managing

As we have seen in this chapter, leaders don't look back to see how many are with them. They aren't concerned with popular opinion, consensus of the masses, or even laws. Ghandi, King, Parks, and many other leaders who stand the test of time broke the laws of the day and spent time in jail. Leaders look to the future, and if what they are doing resonates with us, we follow. Yet you'll also notice that the word "manager" never shows up. That's because the two roles are distinctly different.

Managers have to make sure that people are following. Managers execute the vision and direction that a company's leadership sets. Your job as a manacoach is not to step forward boldly; it's to make sure everyone is on the same page and working together as a great team. So now that leadership has been removed from the equation, let's turn to the next chapter and find out what managing is all about.

# CHAPTER 2 FOLLOW-UP

Moving forward, observe yourself and your actions in considering these five questions:

1.  Do I find myself always analyzing the current situation and asking what future changes could make things better, or am I usually happy with the status quo?

2.  Is it important for me to do the best I possibly can in those things that I'm passionate about?

3.  Am I always looking to do the right thing no matter what others think or say?

4.  Would I do the right thing if it meant breaking a law and going to jail?

5.  Do I prefer to set the course, or do I prefer having the course clearly set for me so I can do a good job in helping the team move forward?

These types of questions are not answered in what you say. They are demonstrated in what you do in determining your level of leadership.

# *c h a p t e r  3*
# THE MANACOACH

*"'Management' isn't the solution, it's the problem. Perhaps it's time to toss the very word 'management' on to the linguistic ash heap alongside 'icebox' and 'horseless carriage.' This era doesn't call for better management; it calls for the renaissance of self-correction."*

## —DANIEL PINK

At a previous, long-ago job, I reported to a new president and CEO named Jim Renahan. One of the high-level managers who Jim inherited when he took the job was the company's primary financial controller. This controller was considered honest and hardworking, and he always worked very long hours. Many times, when I'd return to the office on the weekend after a business trip, I would see the controller diligently working in his office. But a couple of months later, he disappeared. To my surprise, Jim had let him go.

Upon finding this out, I went into Jim's office and asked why. I said that I thought the controller was one of the hardest-working individuals in the office. Although Jim was far too professional to share details, his response was simply that the controller's job was not to work long hours—he was hired to manage a team.

Jim then quickly changed the subject and asked if I could define an extraordinary manager.

I said, "A person who gets things done through other people."

Jim replied, "Close. A great manager is a person who gets things done *efficiently* and *effectively* through other people."

I never forgot his saying that he wasn't impressed with managers who worked long hours on their own. "Kev, if the manager is working long hours because it's crunch time, her whole team better be working at her side, or else the manager is not doing her job."

Sports are popular because, when a team wins, it's poetry in motion. We see teamwork at its best. Everyone on the team knows the plan before they take to the field or ice. They know exactly their position or function and what their role is, in no uncertain terms. They know how they are being measured. They are clear on two things: exactly what they are accountable for and who is going to hold them to account.

In baseball and business, such a person is called a "manager"; in hockey, football, and a number of other sports, he's called a "coach." For the purposes of differentiating a manager from a leader, and agreeing with Daniel Pink, author of *Drive*, that we need a new word for the role, I propose a new name in business for a manager: the "manacoach." Perhaps this renaming will decrease the confusion with a leader's role. We know that the roles of a coach and a manager are the same. They mean exactly the same thing: getting things done *efficiently* and *effectively* through other people. From this point forward, let's say that a manacoach is an extraordinary manager and/or coach.

## The Manacoach Defined

Close your eyes and think of some manacoaches that you've worked with. Specifically, you should be thinking of coaches or managers who really made a difference in your life.

Focus on a great manacoach from a job, a team you played on, a music or drama group you played with, or any type of performance activity where someone was charged with the responsibility of getting *the best out of you*. Now let's rename the person you are thinking of to "Frank" or "Jane," and let's see if I can read your mind and identify some of their character traits.

**Empathy**: This is the ability to read, see into, and/or really understand people. Jane is a master at reading people. She has a toolbox full of techniques, and she knows which one to use on which person. Jane can read people. Empathy oozes out of her, and she always knows what team members are feeling just by looking at them. She knows their emotional buttons, and she knows when and where to push. She is aware that she can destroy a person with a certain tactic, even though the same tactic would get great results with another person.

For example, Jane has two salespeople. Ron is a results-oriented, fast-thinking egomaniac. He's not achieving what he is capable of, so Jane sits down with him, sets a huge goal, and tells Ron that she doesn't think anyone can accomplish it. Ron says he can. Jane argues, identifying all the reasons she doesn't think Ron can do it. However, in the slim chance that Ron can achieve it, Jane will throw a big party for him and apologize in front of everyone for ever doubting him.

Jane knows that this type of strategy would not work with Steve. Steve is relatively new to sales, and right now he needs Jane's support and confidence. As a true manacoach, she knows that the same strategy she used on Ron could kill Steve's motivation and desire to succeed.

**Teacher**: Manacoaches must have the ability to transfer knowledge and concepts. As a manacoach, Frank knows that different people have different ways of learning. He has a library of analogies, so if someone doesn't understand a concept, he uses a different analogy until that person understands. Most of all, he can assess everything a person is doing wrong and can then have the person work on the one thing that magically corrects a number of other issues.

Using an actual teacher as an example, let's show what I mean. A respected mentor and music teacher, Jon Stromquist knew that for students singing or playing wind instruments, the number-one skill set that must be mastered is breathing. Yet by the time we are in grade school, we have subconsciously learned to keep our abdominal muscles tight while we stand erect because this keeps our stomachs from hanging out and making us look fat. Unfortunately, this habit restricts the bottom of our lungs from expanding. Many music teachers either don't know this or don't emphasize it enough. John, though, had a lot of analogies, or "tricks," to make his students relearn how to breathe, such as "Pretend you have a straw in your mouth and it goes right to your stomach." He wouldn't put instruments in children's hands until they breathed properly.

The manacoach identifies and gets people to work on their strengths while disregarding the need to improve upon their weaknesses. Like a true sales professional who knows that if the customer didn't buy it, he didn't sell it, the manacoach knows that if the student didn't learn it, he didn't teach it. Frank also knows that he doesn't have to personally demonstrate how to be effective at a certain skill set. He can get someone else who is better at that skill and develop a mentor relationship.

The true manacoach almost always answers questions with a better question because he knows that people learn better through their own discoveries. Frank knows that great teaching consists of asking great questions. This will be discussed further in chapter 9 on delegation.

**Communicator**: Jane knows that communication cannot take place without trust, so she is always up-front and honest. Every person on her team knows where he or she stands. Jane clearly communicates roles, responsibilities, and expectations. If she has a problem with you or wants to say something critical or negative, she says it to your face. She doesn't hide behind her keyboard, sending memos or e-mails, and she doesn't send another person to tell you. If she can't do it face-to-face, she'll wait—and if she can't wait, it will be done over the phone.

She doesn't talk about others with you, and she doesn't talk about you with others. She knows that communication requires courage. Whether you like it or not, you always know where you stand. It doesn't matter whether or not you like what she is saying; you know that her intentions are only to see you improve. At the same time, it is clear that she isn't out to hurt or humiliate you. Sometimes, when she has had a serious conversation with you because you aren't meeting a critical expectation, she will follow up with a letter just so you are crystal clear on what was discussed and why you aren't meeting expectations. If Jane ends up cutting you from the team, you won't be surprised at all.

**Firm but Just**: Frank is friendly and respectful, but it is always clear that he isn't our friend. He doesn't mix in friendship, because there is a job to be done, and we must be held accountable if the job isn't done up to standards. Regardless of how close we feel to Frank, there is always a line.

Here's an example of how it works. Alan Brown was my second principal when I taught high school. Four times a year, we would get together with the rest of the teachers and spend the day reviewing every student's performance. Afterward, some of us would head to the bar for a beer. Alan would come along, buy the first round, and then leave. Every time. I had a lot of respect for Alan, but we were never friends. The symbolism in his leaving a social function shortly after arriving said it all.

The manacoach defines the standard, and if that is not being met, we will not sustain our current position on the team unless things improve. We know that regardless of how much respect we have for each other, the manacoach will let us go if it doesn't make sense for us to stay.

**Humble**: One of the best things about Jane is that she never takes credit for something a team member achieves, and she always takes full responsibility if a team member, or the team, fails. She owns the fault or the failure—in fact, she blames herself. Her team's success is more important than her own. To get her to take credit for any part of the success is almost impossible.

The manacoach understands that teammates naturally want to grow and do better, so it follows that her role demands the ability to remove barriers for her team.

Perry Niehaus, president of Laser Valley Technology, runs a very successful business on the premise that being humble is a critical ingredient in removing barriers. As Perry says, "If the manacoach comes from a place to service others, she is predisposed to removing barriers. If I come from a place to serve myself first, in my mind, I must create barriers to survive. These barriers come in many forms, including unrealistic or arbitrary rules, complicated procedures and processes, and the inability to understand the importance of keeping things simple."

**Persuasive**: Frank knows how to get things going. He says things that the whole team can relate to so that everyone knows how important it is to succeed. Frank always honors you and your position, but if needed, he will ask questions that get you to rethink your position.

Every manacoach learns that the brightest and most intelligent team member can be either the brightest star or the biggest problem depending on how the manacoach handles his or her objections or issues.

Think back to a time when an incompetent manager announced a new rule, plan, or strategy and wanted you to follow it. It didn't make sense to you, so you asked why, and the response was something like, "Because I said so." How did you feel?

As a manacoach, if you can get the star on your side, you have it made, and if you can't, you are dead. The only way to get that person on your side is to explain the "why" behind your plans when challenged. Responses like, "Because I said so," or "That's the way we have always done it," won't get you anywhere. Persuasion always calls for two steps. First, honor the other person's position to validate the objection. Then ask a question that clarifies why you have chosen your direction.

**Sense of Mission/Goal-Oriented**: There is no doubt in anyone's mind what the goal is. Jane is totally focused on the goal, and she is constantly analyzing the strategies to achieve that goal while also measuring the results of current efforts. Jane clearly and concisely shares what she is building and what she wants it to look like within a certain time line (vision). She explains why it is so important (mission). She makes sure everyone knows how the team's progress is going to be measured (objectives). Everyone knows how it will be accomplished (strategy). Everyone knows the work that has to be done, who will be held accountable, and when their assigned project has to be accomplished (plan).

**Organized**: Along with knowing the strengths and weaknesses of every player, Frank has his team structure written down. Each of the positions exists for a reason, and the roles and responsibilities are clear. From the minute the game starts until the second it ends, everyone knows what their roles and goals are—everyone.

For example, the financial person knows that her primary, overall function is not exposing the assets of the company unnecessarily. That task is broken down into other functions like budgeting, forecasting, analyses, and investments, all in a defined, timely manner. That is much different than the lead salesperson, whose primary, overall function is bringing in new business. That can be broken down into other functions like contacting a defined number of prospects every week, attending planned trade shows, and ensuring that one new client is signed up every month. Every team member knows his or her function on the team.

Frank is constantly using clear and concise data to track improvement. He documents and reviews data and stats. If Frank asks you to do something by a certain time, you can bet your house that he will follow up with you, and it better be done at that time. He is meticulously reliable that way.

**Accountable/Responsible**: Jane doesn't see a difference between these two words. "The buck stops here" is her favorite Harry Truman saying and was John Kennedy's response to the Bay of Pigs fiasco, which caused his popularity to soar. If Jane makes a mistake, she takes full responsibility. She doesn't pass the buck and point fingers at anyone or dodge the arrow. She admits the mistake and asks for forgiveness. If the person Jane is reporting to wants to know who on her team is responsible, Jane always answers with two short words: "I am." For our purposes in this book, "responsibility" and "accountability" are synonyms.

**Vulnerable:** Frank often talks about his fears and about mistakes he has made in the past, and he almost always starts a sentence with, "I need your help." He never brags about himself or pounds his chest. If he's had great accomplishments, you find that out from other sources. Ask him about his greatest challenge growing up, and he'll tell you about a real problem, like living with a loving father who turned into a monster when he drank. When you share one of your weaknesses with him, he shares one of his. Frank knows that power doesn't exist without vulnerability.

As you think about a manacoach that had a great impact on your life, you can come up with some other qualities. Through these skills, characteristics, and talents, as extraordinary manacoaches, Frank and Jane get things done efficiently and effectively through other people.

# THE MANACOACH TEST

This is a good time for you to understand whether or not you want to be a manacoach or what to look for in a manacoach. Evaluate the following statements with real honesty, and check with someone close to you to see if they agree with your responses. If you agree that a statement describes you, give it a ☑. If you don't, mark it with an ☒.

☐ **Empathy:** I am really good at reading and understanding people. I particularly love studying them because I am passionate about figuring out what makes them tick. When I observe people, I watch closely when they are talking to uncover what their expressions and body language are really saying.

- ☐ **Teacher**: I consider myself to be a good educator. I can break an activity down into segments and make people easily comprehend it. I can look at ten things a person is doing wrong and identify the one factor to focus on that will help everything else improve. I love helping people improve.

- ☐ **Communicator:** I communicate my thoughts clearly and in different ways so that different people can understand what I am saying. I'm not afraid to have difficult, face-to-face conversations with team members. My team members can trust what I am saying because they know that my only agenda is to help them grow and move forward.

- ☐ **Firm but Just**: I don't have to be liked by my teammates. I need their respect, and I get it by keeping enough of a line between them and me that everyone knows there are no special arrangements or exceptions for anyone. My teammates know that a friendship with me is difficult because my primary role is to hold them accountable and react appropriately when expectations are not being met.

- ☐ **Humble:** My ego is primarily tied up in helping others grow and succeed. I don't like to be in the limelight. If someone is on the stage getting a trophy, I'm content knowing that I had a hand in helping her get there. I always give credit where credit is due and always take complete responsibility when the team fails. My favorite question is, "Why don't you tell me about your greatest achievement?" If the response is a list of trophies or promotions, I know that I'm dealing with a status-driven individual, and because I'm not into status, I prefer achievement-driven people.

☐ **Persuasive:** I am good at getting others to change their views. I can make people feel safe, and I can find a way to honor their position even though I need to change it. I know how to shape questions in a conversation to invite them to look at things differently. I know that if I'm involved in an argument or fight, I have failed at getting that team member on my side.

☐ **Sense of Mission/Goal-Oriented**: I know the reason behind the goal, and I am always focused on that goal. I have one major goal for the team, and we all know what it is, because I never let anyone forget it. Leaders always look at new ideas and want to take different directions, but I must keep the team focused on the goal and the strategies that will work.

☐ **Organized:** I am organized and highly prepared for anything. I realize that being on time is a commitment, and my ability to keep commitments determines my level of integrity with others on the team. "A place for everything and everything in its place" is my motto, and everyone knows that if I ask them to do something, I will follow up and hold them accountable.

☐ **Accountable/Responsible**: I don't point fingers. I take full responsibility when something goes wrong because I'm in charge of the team.

☐ **Vulnerable**: I acknowledge that being vulnerable, acknowledging what keeps me up at night, and admitting my weaknesses are all strengths.

Now, you might be asking why I didn't ask you to score your responses with a range, like one to ten, especially when your responses to ten statements would easily add up to a percentage. The reason is that the true manacoach has *all* of these traits. They are all interdependent, just like the three legs of a stool or the links in a chain. A two-legged stool is not functional even though it has a passing grade of 67 percent. A hundred-link chain is no longer functional if even one link is dysfunctional.

Therefore, on the responses where you didn't get a ☑, you need to ask yourself if you are capable of getting there. For example, it would be difficult to be a manacoach if one gets an ☒ on statements eight and nine—can that person become more organized and take responsibility? If the answer is no, then training that person to be a manacoach is no more likely to be successful than teaching someone who isn't a people person to be a salesperson.

Can you work on these traits and improve? Definitely. But the point is, should you? As Marcus Buckingham points out over and over again in *First Break All the Rules*, shouldn't you take on tasks that better fit your true talents? I'll level with you. I've tried managing people in the past, and I fall short. If I'm totally honest with myself, it's because my weakness falls in statement number eight. After years of running into walls and spending time with the right coaches (and therapists), I finally realized that I should hire others to keep me organized.

---

## Understanding Your Results

So before continuing in this book, you need to be brutally honest with yourself. If you are, you will save yourself and—more important— a lot of others substantial grief and suffering. You have to identify which of the following you are reading the rest of this book to do:

1.   Become or improve as a manacoach OR

2.   Understand the traits of a manacoach so you can help one grow OR

3.   Find or identify a manacoach for your organization

Now let's compare the attributes of a great leader to those of a great manager. If it's in a gray box, it's not a necessary attribute, and it's just there for comparison. If it is in white, it is a required attribute:

| LEADER | MANAGER |
|---|---|
| Vision | *Vision* |
| *Organized* | Organized |
| *Empathetic* | Empathetic |
| Sense of Mission | Sense of Mission |
| *Teacher* | Teacher |
| Determined | Determined |
| Disciplined | *Disciplined* |
| Focused | Focused |
| Honest | Honest |
| *Persuasive* | Persuasive |
| *Communicator* | Communicator |
| Ground Breaker | *Ground Breaker* |
| Integrity | Integrity |
| Does the right thing | Does things efficiently and effectively through others |
| Does things efficiently and effectively | |

## Differences Explained

It's important to define these character traits so that you can truly understand the difference between a leader and a manacoach.

**Vision:** Read anything about leaders and you will see an infatuation with progressing forward. Leaders are visionaries, completely focused on the future. They know where they are going, and they know how and why they are going there. The manacoach is focused on implementing a winning strategy to achieve the desired vision. The manacoach needs to understand the leader's vision.

**Organized:** Leaders don't have to be organized. In fact, most leaders admit that they aren't. They are often thinking and dreaming—some call it attention deficit disorder, and it makes me cry that we attempt to numb that talent with drugs. Leaders must be confident that their manacoach is going to have the right things in place at the right time. They also know that when their manacoach assigns something, she is going to organize herself so that she follows up.

**Empathetic:** Leaders don't have to understand people—in fact, they often don't. Remember, people follow leaders because of their cause. If people share the cause, they are following not for the leader but for themselves. If you do an Internet search of the top ten modern leaders of all time, Steve Jobs often shows up. However, one would be hard pressed to find anyone who worked with him describe him as empathetic.

**Teacher:** Leaders teach through demonstration. If we want to be like them, we observe and attempt to replicate. As Malcolm Gladwell convinces us with a multitude of examples supported by hard data in his book *Blink: The Power of Thinking Without Thinking*, one must conclude that leaders are more often than not unable to teach or coach, because they are totally unaware of what makes them great. The manacoach can look at what a team member is doing wrong and pick out the one thing that, if corrected, will improve all the other things. If you take a lesson from a manacoach and you leave that lesson confused, you need to find another manacoach.

**Disciplined:** Viktor Frankl has the best definition of discipline that I have read to date: "the ability to do the unnatural." It's not natural to brush your teeth; it takes discipline to brush them every day. It's not natural to run for five miles, swim a mile, or spend ninety minutes in a hot room with fifty other people doing yoga while you sweat all over each other. These things take discipline, and leaders have it. An amateur practices a skill until they get it right. A professional practices a skill until she can't do it wrong. Think of a leader as a professional. Think of the discipline it takes to hit a thousand tennis balls or swim four miles a day. Leaders have discipline, and the manacoach makes sure the leaders are doing the right things, have the best equipment, and are in the best environment to practice.

I credit one of my great coaches, Agnes Mura, for asking me the difference between being organized and being disciplined. The manacoach is organized. If the goal for the team is to swim a mile in a record time, the manacoach organizes the pool time, makes sure the transportation is arranged, and has the necessary equipment and trainers in place. But the leader is disciplined. She gets up and out every day and swims the miles because she knows that she must if she is to achieve some goal in the future that involves strong swimming ability. She has discipline and the ability to do the unnatural.

**Persuasive:** Leaders don't have to persuade us to follow them. We follow them because their thinking, or what they believe, is always consistent with their thoughts and actions, and so we trust them. Manacoaches never argue with you or tell you what to do, like a boss. They have a way of honoring your position and then asking questions to make you think. They have all sorts of questions, analogies, and stories up their sleeve that prompt you to understand. They can answer the why behind anything they are asking you to do. The manacoach is a master at the power of persuasion through questions that make you think.

**Communicator:** Would you agree that Helen Keller was a leader? She was the perfect example of leading through example because she couldn't talk. She communicated through her actions. How about Abraham Lincoln, who was an introvert who stuttered? So leaders don't necessarily have to be good communicators, because their actions speak louder than words, but the manacoach does. If we agree that a manacoach gets things done efficiently and effectively through others, then doesn't it follow that the art of communication is critical? How could a manacoach function if she doesn't communicate both clearly and concisely?

**Groundbreaker:** I love this term because it speaks for itself. Think back to any great accomplishment by a leader, whether it's the discovery of bacteria many years ago or the invention of the microchip. There was a leap from the way everyone else thinks to a discovery of a simple solution. And more times than not, the groundbreaking solution was not accepted by the masses and the groundbreaker suffered. Leaders are groundbreakers. When McDonald's is looking for someone to buy and run a restaurant, they are not looking for a groundbreaking visionary, entrepreneur, or leader. They are looking for a manacoach. They don't want this person to change anything. They are looking for someone who can get things done as the current game is played, efficiently and effectively through others.

## An Example of a Leader versus a Manacoach

Using this list, let's examine the famous individual we identified when discussing empathy—the late Steve Jobs of Apple. He was a visionary who knew exactly what he wanted and would settle for nothing less. Nor was his success a fluke, because he took his leadership skills to Pixar and enjoyed the same level of success, which he further demonstrated when he returned to Apple. Determined, disciplined, focused, honest, groundbreaking, integrity, "does the right thing," and "gets things done efficiently and effectively" all are traits that come up in writings about him. Few would argue that Steve Jobs wasn't a great leader.

How does Jobs rate as a manacoach? Let's look at the list. He might or might not have been organized, but plenty of evidence shows that his empathy was weak. And that is a critical attribute for a manacoach. Nothing in the literature shows that he was good with people, a great teacher, or a great communicator. Nobody would question his impressive abilities as a leader, but he did not have the skill set of a manacoach.

For years I have suffered frustration when even the best authorities use "leadership" and "management" as synonyms. In fact, these two roles' true character traits and inherent skill sets lie at opposite ends of the spectrum.

If we agree that a great manacoach gets things done efficiently and effectively through others, does he have to make a lot of sales in order to produce great salespeople? If a manacoach is responsible for producing great golfers, does she have to be able to hit the ball well? Why does a manacoach need to have vision or the ability to see into the future? Isn't his goal to produce better people and properly implement a well-thought-out game plan?

A leader can adopt the go-it-alone approach. A manacoach needs others to direct as part of a team. All the manacoach qualities discussed in this chapter are people-oriented qualities. In order for you to be a manacoach, you need to be able to connect with people.

# CHAPTER 3 FOLLOW-UP

Consider the questions posed in the previous "Manacoach Test." If you answered no to some of the characteristics, could you answer yes in the future? Ask others who know you well if they agree with your answers. We can't see ourselves through our own eyes!

*c h a p t e r  4*

# DOES A STAR MAKE A GOOD MANAGER?

*"The true genius of a great manager is his or her ability to individualize. A great manager is one who understands how to trip each person's trigger."*

## —MARCUS BUCKINGHAM

Manacoaches have a far-reaching influence over others. Yet just because they can achieve amazing things as an individual doesn't rule out the possibility of them destroying others' potential with lightning speed. When Marcus Buckingham says that manacoaches know how to "trip each person's trigger," he is saying that they "get" people. So the question is this: If you are really good at what you do, does that mean you understand what makes you great? Does that mean you can relate or teach it to someone else so that she can do it well?

Although we see teams perform together in activities such as theater, music, and business, sports are a great way to illustrate this point because we have a long history and vast amounts of hard data to use when analyzing great players and great coaches in team sports history. Let's look at some sports stars and see how a top performer can inadvertently destroy the future potential of some really talented individuals.

## What Makes Them Great?

How many young players and coaches did Andre Agassi confuse when he told everyone who would listen that he got so much top spin because he rotated his wrist just before he hit the ball? Because of Andre's position as a world-renowned and extremely popular professional tennis player, thousands of tennis amateurs would listen to his every word. As I read Malcolm Gladwell's book *Blink*, all I could think about were the victims—all of those young players and their coaches who took Agassi's advice and hit thousands of balls, trying to duplicate his topspin by flicking their wrist before they hit the ball. They couldn't understand why they didn't get the expected result.

Imagine their reaction years later, when digital imaging could slow the action of hitting the ball down to a point where they could tell that Agassi's wrist actually did not turn until *after* he hit the ball. How many potentially great tennis players did Agassi send on a wild goose chase with this inaccurate advice? Don't get me wrong. I admire Agassi for his accomplishments, and I don't question his intentions in giving this erroneous advice, because he really thought he was right. But it doesn't change the fact that we listened because he was an internationally acclaimed tennis player. Like so many other leaders he was undeniably great, *but like many leaders, he didn't know what made him great.*

The same principle applies to the all-time greatest hockey player, Wayne Gretzky. They call him "The Great One." He was a highly skilled player and was humble, modest, and generous to a fault. He understood that he played on a team, and he passed the puck countless times when he had an opportunity to score. He would pass to his teammates because he knew that most goalies expected the player in front to take the shot, and lightning-quick thinking and surprise is the name of the game. He constantly put the team first, like any great player in any arena.

He learned at an early age to develop strength on his weak side, and when he hit the big leagues, the poor goalie watching him charge was totally unable to predict which side Gretzky would come in on. He would make unexplainable passes behind him without looking. Many of us felt that he must have eyes in the back of his head. I don't have to convince anyone of the gift and the "magic" that this person brought to hockey when he stepped on the ice as a *leader*.

But in October 2005, Wayne Gretzky stepped back into the arena not as a leader but as the head coach of the Phoenix Coyotes. A great player should be an effective coach, right? With only a hypothesis at the time and no research to back it, I often stated (solely based on years of personal experience and observations in working with teams and business owners) that he only had a 20 percent chance of becoming a successful coach. I publicly predicted that he would fail.

As it turned out, Wayne had four terrible seasons as a coach. Some speculate that he would have been fired in his first year if he wasn't part owner of the team. Why did I think the odds were stacked against his becoming a successful coach? Because in my years of coaching performance activities like music, volleyball, basketball, and business, I have witnessed the same obstacles over and over again. And now, we finally have hard research to back these observations.

## Who Is a Better Coach?

Let me ask: if you are looking for someone to coach you in golf, which teacher would you choose?

Fred won five state finals. While on tour, Fred was among the top hundred finalists in four majors. He is a true leader in golf. Now let's consider Barbara. She never qualified to play on the tour. To get a professional license, she had to work very hard on lifting the ball out of the sand. She never won a tournament of any kind. Yet after only four years of coaching ten serious students, three have won high school championships, and one has won a state championship. Compare her results to Fred, who after fourteen years of coaching has yet to produce a notable student.

When deciding who to pick as a golf coach, you have a far better chance of learning golf properly if you choose Barbara. Yet if all you knew was that Fred was a proven winner and Barbara wasn't, traditionally you pick the better player every time—the leader.

If I asked who you wanted a lesson from, Rory McIlroy or Barbara, both you and I would instantly choose Rory. It seems to just make sense, yet it's actually the opposite of sense. We are making the common, erroneous assumption that because a leader has overcome competitive pressure and achieved good results, he or she must know how to teach or coach us and hold us accountable.

We don't know if Rory is a good coach. If you choose him over Barbara to teach your child, you will have a lot of bragging rights, but according to the results of our research, there is also a 4:1 chance that you just did your child a significant disservice. The same principle applies in business. In our business units, many more times than not, why do we choose Fred or Rory as our manacoach and overlook Barbara altogether?

## Running the Numbers on Players and Coaches

Many years ago, I started thinking: if business is a performance activity, and managers and coaches are both charged with the same responsibility of getting things done *efficiently* and *effectively* through others, then why not take a look at a few popular team sports played in North America to see what the data shows? More specifically, I wanted to know what happens when a professional team chooses a leader as its manacoach based solely on his or her ability to perform.

So my team of researchers and I embarked on a major endeavor to find out what happened to top professional athletes who then became professional coaches. We started by analyzing and collecting data on top coaches to see where they ranked as players. It was unanimously decided that one sport was not enough to ensure accurate results. After careful consideration we chose three team sports with a long history: ice hockey, baseball, and basketball. All three sports have detailed statistics recorded over time, so we could compile accurate totals.

## Ice Hockey

When focusing on the National Hockey League, we decided to use the Elo rating method, because it most consistently identified the all-time top players. The Elo rating system is a method for calculating the relative skill levels of players in competitor-versus-competitor games. A player's Elo rating is represented by a number that increases or decreases based upon the outcome of games between rated players. After every game, the winning player takes points from the losing one. The difference between the ratings of the winner and loser determines the total number of points gained or lost after a game. In using this method, we were able to identify fifty all-time top professional hockey players.

Out of those fifty players, seventeen would go on to professionally coach. This included Wayne Gretzky, who was ranked second on the scale of all-time great players, Larry Robinson (ranked eighth), Phil Esposito (ranked ninth), and Bryan Trottier (ranked fourteenth).

It's generally accepted that good coaches, including those considered to be manacoaches, have a win/lose record of .5 or greater in a season. In other words, .49 means they lose more games than they win, and .51 means they win more games than they lose. Out of the seventeen of the top fifty players of all time who went on to coach hockey at the professional level, how many do you think ended up with a winning record? If you guessed a lowly *three*, you are correct.

So if you chose a hockey coach based exclusively on his ability to perform in hockey, you would have a less than one in five chance of making the correct decision, or 17.65 percent, to be exact. Of the very best four players—Esposito, Gretzky, Robinson, and Trottier— only Esposito had a winning record in coaching, posting a .533—but he coached for only two seasons. Gretzky, Robinson, and Trottier failed. In fact, Robinson and Trottier didn't last through their first season. Gretzky lasted four years, but it is speculated that he would have lasted only one if he didn't own part of the team.

To find really successful coaches, we had to expand our focus to the top-hundred Elo-ranked hockey players. That list includes Dit Clapper (ranked seventy-ninth) and Toe Blake (ranked sixty-seventh). Dit Clapper, at a .530 record, coached for only four years. But Toe Blake maintained a .634 winning average over fourteen years of coaching, taking the Montreal Canadiens to eight League and eight Stanley Cup championships. It's interesting to note that only one out of the top hundred players of all time in hockey repeatedly took his team to a national final as a manacoach!

## Basketball

Top players in the National Basketball Association do better in coaching than their NHL counterparts but nowhere near enough to undermine our assumption. Out of the top fifty basketball players of all time, sixteen would become coaches, and four had a winning average of .51 or more. Wilt Chamberlain, ranked second, coached for only a year and lost two out of three games. He quit after that season because he was "bored." Magic Johnson, ranked sixth, coached his team to a mere five losses and one win before he quit early in the season. Thank goodness for Larry Bird, ranked as the ninth best player, who won more than two-thirds of his games as coach. He was chosen as coach of the year in 1997, and he manacoached his team to the Eastern Conference championship in 2000.

Despite Larry Bird's stellar example as a manacoach, the odds against a top-hundred player taking his team to a conference final were 99:1. If you calculate the coaches out of the top hundred players of all time just in terms of winning more games than he lost, the odds are 4:1 against you.

## Baseball

In looking at Major League Baseball, we adopted a different set of criteria. We evaluated managers from 1990 and forward, and we looked at both those who were retired players and those who never played professionally. First, we identified all the managers who had played professional baseball (eighty-five managers). Those who coached for less than 162 games were deleted from the study (a full season is 162 games). This resulted in sixty-three managers.

In baseball, a player's WAR score (Wins Above Replacement) is an accepted way of identifying good players; a player with a

WAR score of above .8 is deemed to be an above-average player. We evaluated the thirty-six managers whose WAR scores were below .8. Of this group, fourteen (39 percent) were successful manacoaches, winning more games than they lost. Of the twenty-seven managers whose WAR scores were over .8, fourteen (52 percent) were successful. So of the sixty-three qualifying managers, the odds were only 13 percent in your favor if you picked the player with the better WAR score.

We then examined the success rate of coaches who didn't play professional baseball at all, and we were sent into a state of shock. Of the seventeen who never played professionally, eight (47 percent) were successful manacoaches. That 47 percent is not far shy of the 52 percent of above-average players who went on to manage successfully. In other words, the ones who never played at the major league level were nearly as likely to be successful as the ones who did.

For years I have argued with clients attempting to convince them that great managers do not need to have played the game to be able to coach it. I have one engineering company that still thinks it cannot put a person into a position of management unless that person has the technical expertise. The data simply does not support this way of thinking.

To sum up, the three groups break down like this:

Group 1: Twenty-seven above-average baseball players produced fourteen winning managers.

Group 2: Thirty-six below-average baseball players produced fourteen winning managers.

Group 3: Seventeen who never played produced eight winning managers.

Whether we are talking baseball, basketball, hockey, or most likely any other performance-based activity—and that includes business—

it is clear that picking a person to manage a team based solely on their ability to perform stacks the odds of choosing a candidate who will be successful at up to 4:1 against you. So the question is now: what should we look for when choosing a manacoach?

## Why Doesn't Business Reward the Players?

Our results conclusively show that top manacoaches should not be selected based on how skilled they are in performing the activity in question. Yet in thousands of businesses, the way to become a manacoach is to perform well at your job. Why do we keep making this mistake in business?

When Wayne Gretzky was playing at his prime, he didn't want Glen Sather's job as head coach. Why? Consider that Gretzky got more money, more recognition, and more status as the top performer on the team than he would have as head coach. It's only in business that we've gotten confused and forgotten that managing is a team performance activity.

One reason for this mistake is that in business, our leaders are incentivized to want to be manacoaches. If you are a top player in baseball, you get paid far more than the manager. The top player also gets far more perks and recognition as well. But in almost all businesses, that's not the case. In business, managers get more of all of these perks than the people doing the actual work that drives the results.

In business we see climbing to the top not as getting better at what we do. Unfortunately, we want to become the top manacoach. This is true even though, as clearly shown in the research, a top performer has very little chance of possessing the talents and characteristics required to be a winning manacoach.

Allow me to put this in as simple terms as possible. The talents of a leader are extremely different than those of a manacoach. Attempting to get a manacoach to take on leadership roles or getting leaders to take on the roles of a manacoach is like expecting a duck to fly like an eagle or an eagle to swim like a duck. It won't happen; they are wired differently.

As the late Stephen Covey said so eloquently, the leaders do the right things, and the manacoaches do things right—specifically, getting things done efficiently and effectively through others. So now, if this makes sense to you, let's spend the rest of the book talking about the skill sets and characteristics of a manacoach—not a leader.

# CHAPTER 4 FOLLOW-UP

If you find yourself troubled with accepting a top player as a "leader," ask yourself this:

1.   Is the top performer on a team based on his or her very results not always looking to the future in the game and in developing better plans, strategies, or solutions?

2.   In the end, isn't it true that the top performers only do what they are told if it makes sense?

3.   How could they be the "leader" of the pack if they weren't disciplined and determined?

4.   If they are so good at what they do, and they lead the pack, why do leaders have such a high failure rate at getting things done efficiently and effectively through others?

*chapter 5*

# CULTURE AND THE MANACOACH

*"If your culture doesn't like geeks, you are in real trouble."*

## —BILL GATES

Jane is a manacoach who challenges her people. She loves it when one of her team members goes above and beyond. She is organized, which is one reason she was the top manacoach in her last position at a large company. They loved her passion for growing people and her ability to produce great teams.

Yet Jane is also an introverted, detail-oriented people person, and she does not like going to work with her new company. She works in a sales department where everyone is loud, boisterous, crude, and rude. Jane prefers a more quiet and professional environment, like the mechanical engineering firm she worked at before she was forced to leave when her husband was transferred. In her current position, she especially doesn't like the practice of lying to and misleading the customer just to "get the deal done."

When Jane complained to the owner of the business, he agreed that it's not right, but he didn't do anything about it. Jane thinks

51

she can change the company's culture, but in reality, she only has one of two choices. She can continue to dislike her environment but tolerate it, or she should leave.

If you want to become a better manacoach, it's important that you understand your company's culture. If the culture doesn't align with your beliefs, no matter how good you are or how much you try, the reality is that you will never succeed.

## What Is Culture?

The million-dollar question is, "What is culture?" Everyone has a different answer. In addition to being difficult to define, culture is difficult to see unless you know what you are looking for.

For a good part of my life, I spent a lot of time researching the word "culture," looking for a clear and simple definition that would satisfy my understanding. I was becoming increasingly frustrated when I finally asked a business professor at Royal Roads University: "What is culture?"

He quickly responded with two words: *it's everything.* Fireworks went off in my brain like I had just discovered a cure for cancer. He was right.

It's what you see, hear, smell, and feel when you visit a country, company, institution, organization, or any group of people. A culture's roots originated with its founder(s), and the older, stronger, and more defined the culture is, the more difficult it is to change. Depending on the culture, it may only be changeable from the bottom up—that's how strongly entrenched it can become over time. We see this in politics when a new president of a country tries and fails to change gun laws due to the right to bear arms being entrenched in the culture. The same behavior that is accepted in one culture could get one arrested in another. I have gay clients who are encouraged to bring their partners or spouses to company events, and nobody thinks anything of it. Yet in other cultures, these same individuals would be harassed, assaulted, or even arrested and executed for showing their affection for each other.

In short, culture is "everything." When you join a defined group of people, it's the scent in the air, the noise level, the energy you feel, the speed that everyone moves at, the humor or lack of it, the interactions . . . it's everything you take in through your senses. Once I got my head wrapped around that professor's definition, so many things about working with management teams became clear.

As a manacoach, you know what you believe to be right. These are your values, which determine what you will and won't tolerate. Values can be identified by what you personally believe to be right, true, and good. You need to be cognizant of what you value to ensure that your values align with your company's culture.

Identifying the traits held by a group of people and breaking them down to a few core values results in a list that defines the group's culture. For example, if you observe that a culture is happy and playful, and the staff is always upbeat and smiling, the core value might be "fun." It's not right or wrong. It could work for one person and not for another, which is why it is important to not make any judgments when identifying values. Working in a geek culture or a serious, get-things-done culture is not right or wrong—it just is. There is only one important question you must ask yourself after you've clearly identified a culture's core values: *do the core values of that culture resonate and align with your beliefs?*

I remember working with Dan Millman, speaker and author of *Way of the Peaceful Warrior,* and someone kept asking him about his religious beliefs. He simply responded with, "I'm not sure about religious beliefs, but I do know that I no longer believe in right or wrong—I just believe in consequences." If you start working for a company where the daily office environment consists of everyone laughing and playing jokes on each other, you might survive but you won't thrive if you believe everyone should be focused and serious when they are at work.

Why is it that in some companies, everyone is prepared to roll up their sleeves and sweep the floor if that is what's required to get the job done, while in other companies, there are individuals who wouldn't even consider the thought of picking up a mop because it's "beneath" them? These are two prime examples of different, highly defined cultures, and you will almost never see either of them change.

I worked with a manufacturing company whose president would constantly grab a broom or help in inventory counts if that was required at the time. Everyone in that company followed the president's example and was always willing to help with any situation. In fact, one of his core value statements was, "Everyone is prepared to push a broom."

I have also worked with companies where individuals hold the belief that because they went to college for eight years, they should never have to pick up a mop again. Even if their help is desperately needed at the time, they are just not going to do it. However, those individuals who refuse to sweep or mop are still very good employees—engineers or accountants, for example. They were hired because they are exceptional at what they do, and that is where they like to roll up their sleeves and focus on their contribution to the company. Again, this view is not right or wrong—it just *is*.

Bill Gates is right that if someone is considering working at a tech company and doesn't like geeks, he or she is likely in the wrong place. Take a stroll through any organization and allow your senses to take in "everything." You will "feel" the culture.

I have been asked by many manacoaches in large companies to come in and assist in building their team's culture as a way of improving the overall company's culture. I refuse these types of requests, because no matter how good the manacoach might be, the overall culture will prevail.

Take, for example, a large mining company where the manacoach wanted to redefine the culture for everyone in his supply chain division, with the hope that the change would spread through the rest of the company once everyone witnessed the overall positive impact. The idea sounds great, but the overall culture, established by the founder, will inevitably prevail. The manacoach in question needs to find another culture that is more aligned with his core values.

Imagine joining Southwest Airlines as a manacoach and attempting to make your team act in a more serious manner. Your thinking is, "People are already anxious about flying, and we need to show them that we take it seriously." Your team at Southwest is going to think, "You need to find another place to work."

Herb Kelleher, founder of Southwest Airlines, talks about receiving a letter from Diane von Fürstenberg, the iconic Belgian-American fashion designer, who said she didn't like Southwest's "ambiance." When von Fürstenberg said she didn't like Southwest's "ambiance," she was saying that she didn't like their "culture." Kelleher wrote back, stating that he "didn't know what ambiance was, [he] was just damn glad to hear that [they] had one."

The point is if you don't like the humor, camaraderie, and casual culture at Southwest, you had best not have anything to do with them, because it's ingrained in their culture. It's not right or wrong. Some people, like von Fürstenberg, think flying is serious business, and if that's what you think, you shouldn't fly with Southwest. And if you are a manacoach who shares von Fürstenberg's values, you shouldn't work for them, because you are not going to change the culture.

Search Google for "you can't change culture," and you will see the tremendous amount of research on this subject. Have certain leaders managed to enact change in a culture? Definitely—but we are speaking to you as a manacoach. What is your role as a manacoach? It's to get things done efficiently and effectively through others who are members of that particular culture.

## Status over Achievement

One critical core value worth examining is the importance of status versus achievement, best illustrated in Patrick Lencioni's book *The Five Temptations of a CEO*. While advising hundreds of management teams over the past three decades, I have found that manacoaches should be strictly achievement-based. They should have no time or desire for status. Titles should mean nothing to them. Manacoaches are only concerned with the success and well-being of the team. When interviewing people, manacoaches make a point of asking for examples of achievement. They listen carefully to the response.

Does a person consider achievement to be something like a promotion up the ladder or acceptance to a special group or club, or do they consider achievement to mean actually accomplishing something or bringing something to completion? Was most of their answer focused on the trophy, ribbon, or reward? "I was named captain of the team." "I have an MBA." "I had the best office in the building." "Visit my trophy room, and I will show you what I've accomplished." Or was their achievement actually doing something significant for the good of others or the organization? Here are achievement-type responses that identify the difference:

- "I was bringing the ball up the field, I saw the man open, and I knew that he would have a better chance of putting it in, so I passed it to him."

- "I knew that there was one person holding out, and if I could get her on our side, we could close the deal. I spent days researching what could change her position. I found it, delivered it, and our team closed the biggest deal in its history."

Some cultures are riddled with status-based individuals, who are usually very political and do not achieve very much at all. Everyone wants to climb the ladder, and if they have to climb over a fellow team member to get to the top, then so be it.

As you read that last sentence, perhaps you are picturing status-based managers you worked for in the past, and just thinking of them makes your skin crawl. They took credit for everything when it was a win, and they blamed you and others when it was a loss. They were focused on themselves first. They would cuddle up to those they considered important, and they ignored those they considered beneath them. They would talk and would not listen. They were self-centered and only concerned about themselves and their status. Their favorite word was "I" or "me," and they only used the word "we" if it could make them look good or if the team failed at something. They created barriers so others would have to come to them, as opposed to removing barriers so the team could achieve more with less effort. If this type of culture exists, look to the very top, and you will find a status-based individual defining the culture.

In order for you to be effective as a manacoach, your core values must be aligned with the culture's values. If this is not the case, you have no choice but to leave and find a culture that values what you believe to be right, true, and good. You might survive in a culture where your core values don't align, but you won't thrive. You won't be achieving your full potential, because what you have to offer is not valued.

## Are You Trapped as a Manacoach?

I thank my friend Nicholas Economou (entrepreneur, time management guru, and business coach extraordinaire) for teaching me the meaning of a trap. It's very simple, but don't let simple fool you in terms of depth of meaning: "a trap is something you are not prepared or able to walk or get away from." Identify something or someone you are not prepared or able to walk away from, and that's a trap for you. If you are not aligned with the values of your current culture and you are not prepared to walk away, you are trapped. A trap is not necessarily a negative thing. Some traps you don't want to walk away from, like your children, your family, a friend, or a piece of property you really like. But it's critically important to know what traps are so you can strategize your options and better predict possible outcomes.

If you value all of the talents you have to offer, and your current culture does not align with your values, why on earth would you want to spend time in a place where what you have to offer is not appreciated?

## What Do I Look for When I'm Hiring?

"Can I change the culture that I'm in?" This is a good question, and if you have a simple answer, then you don't understand the question. As the company's founder, Herb Kelleher established the core values of Southwest Airlines. If he hired you as its CEO and you went in with the intention of changing the culture, you would fail. The core values were ingrained and understood. When you are offered a position at any company, you should do everything you can to understand its culture before taking the job, because no matter what you hope, you are not going to change that culture.

Reviewing a company's stated core values would be a good place to start, but keep in mind that the vast majority of companies in North America don't have their core values in writing, and if they do, their statements are platitudes, misunderstood, and not followed by all. You may find that words like "honesty," "integrity," and "professional" cause the individuals in the organization to give a blank stare. That should raise the caution flag for you. You may want to probe further, looking for the unspoken core values.

Travel through Germany, and then take a trip through Mexico. If you were to come up with a core value statement for Germany, it might be "a place for everything, and everything in its place." Deadlines are deadlines, everyone must stand in line and wait their turn, and if something's not perfect, it doesn't go out. You feel it when you walk into one of their airports or when you exit a train. "Matter of fact," "orderly," and "rigid" are terms that might come to mind in describing the German culture.

Now consider Mexico. The word that might come to mind is "mañana." Afternoon naps when the sun is hot, or *siestas*, are something you would not see in Germany. In Mexican culture, lines are for those who don't know a shortcut or have a friend or relative that can get you to the front of the line. In Mexican culture, relationships and family are paramount. They are important in Germany, but they come second to doing a good job and being the best you can be.

Yes, these are great exaggerations, and there are always exceptions. We must suspend judgment because neither culture is right or wrong. But if you like what you hear about Germany, you should go work in that country; if you feel you are more aligned with Mexico, then go work and live in that culture. The important point is to truly understand the culture before you make your choice.

I use countries as an example, but the same can be said about every organization. There is a unique culture in every organization where behavior is consistent with preexisting values.

Every business should have a proven process for identifying its culture, but unfortunately, most don't. Some companies have attempted to go through the process and have their values written on their wall, in their boardroom, and in their employee manual, but nobody lives them, and the real culture can be completely different than what the company wishes it were.

It's almost impossible for you, as a manacoach, to clearly identify the true, core values of an organization until you dive into it headfirst. Only from being inside, over time, can you start to truly identify what values are deeply held by the culture.

For example, one of my core values is that disruption with good intent is critical for growth. The only way I can truly evaluate this in a company is to get inside and wait for a situation where an employee challenges the person who holds him or her accountable. If that never happens, I'm in a culture that will not fit me. By a different measure, if the employee is shot down immediately, without an opportunity to respond, or they won't respond out of fear, I'm also in the wrong culture.

Another way to evaluate the culture of an organization is to meet the founder(s), even though you should realize that this is not always possible. If the company has not been merged with another company, it will usually value what the founder values (or valued). When I'm helping a company's top management team (often referred to as "leadership" or "executive" team), we work hard to help the founder identify the core values. During the exercise, I make sure that the team realizes the founder will have the final say, because they are the *founder's* core values. In other words, the founder will have the trump card simply because what is near and dear to the founder is already established in the company's culture.

Although you will have to jump in to really understand a culture, you don't always have to jump in headfirst. Does the company have its core values identified, and are its people living them? Asking for the values will give you an indication, and it can be telling to ask questions that can bring up real-life examples of how they handled or would handle various situations.

Can you spend a couple of days or weeks in the culture (on a trial basis) to get an idea of whether your values align with the culture's? If you are currently employed, perhaps you can take unpaid leave to spend time in this new culture. Can you spend some time with the founders, so that you can observe both what they profess to value and how they actually behave?

Whatever your answer is, know this: if you officially enter a culture with values that are in conflict with your values, you are or will end up trapped, and it's impossible to thrive that way.

You will know when you are in conflict with your current culture's values, but you may not want to believe it. However, nothing good ever comes from denial. In order for you not to be in denial, you must both know and believe that you are in a culture that does not fit your values, and you must make plans to exit it, because you won't change it.

# CHAPTER 5 FOLLOW-UP

1.   Now that you know the definition of a culture, has your workplace identified the core values (what the organization agrees to be right, true, and good) that describe your culture, and does everyone in your culture understand them?

2.   Are the core value statements simple, descriptive, easy to understand, and easy to explain to others?

3.   Do you fit in your current culture or are you trapped?

4.   Does your culture hire, fire, reward, and recognize everyone based on your core values so that they are constantly reinforced?

*c h a p t e r   6*

# THERE IS NO POWER WITHOUT VULNERABILITY

*"Security is mostly a superstition. It does not exist in nature, nor do the children of men as a whole experience it. Avoiding danger is no safer in the long run than outright exposure. Life is either a daring adventure, or nothing."*

**—HELEN KELLER**

Many years ago I took a weekend workshop. Although it felt sort of cultish, I was amazed at how the seminar leader, within the first couple of hours, was able to coax people up onto the stage to share their most intimate experiences. He then said something that I will never forget: "You can't be truly powerful unless you are willing to be vulnerable."

That quote made me squint in confusion. What in the world was that supposed to mean? Yet it started me on a journey that has lasted to this day.

A year later, I came upon a TED talk regarding vulnerability. On June 12, 2010, Dr. Brené Brown appeared at the University of Houston to present the findings from her research on the concept of vulnerability to a TEDx audience.

That first twenty-minute presentation would change Brown's and many others' lives (including mine) forever. It transferred her data-backed findings from the classroom to the world. That video now has tens of millions of views on TED.com, YouTube, and other media outlets. For many of us, that video is one of the most powerful, thought-provoking presentations ever seen on TED.com. Unfortunately, for many others, it means nothing.

I saw Brown's presentation on TED.com a couple of months after it was shot. Having recovered from my confusion at the weekend workshop, I was even more fascinated, because now Dr. Brown was saying that she found that the people who were strong enough to be vulnerable were "wholehearted" people. That view is in contrast to how vulnerability is regarded in many societies, where it is seen as weakness. Brown's findings were saying the exact opposite.

Think back to some of your great bosses, coaches, or teachers— people who really affected you in a positive way. Were they curious, or were they know-it-alls? Did they relate to a challenge of yours by sharing how they had the same type of struggles, or did they make you feel like you were the only one on the planet who had this problem?

When I was coaching a new facilitator in his first year, he confessed that he was really struggling. I could instantly see his relief when I shared with him that my first year was the most difficult year of my life. It is for everyone. Learning is so much more fun and effective when there is no fear of failure. If you learn that the person who is teaching you also had the same kinds of struggles in the beginning, the intimidation factor disappears, doesn't it?

Since then I have shown Brown's TEDx video to thousands of business owners, managers, and human resources (HR) people. I especially like showing it to small management teams and then asking them to identify the one message they got out of it. The responses are amazing because they are so very different. I have witnessed everything from complete emotional breakdowns to people who turn to me afterward and say, "I don't know why we are watching this. What does this have to do with managing people?"

You have to be passionate about your company's products to be a great sales rep, but as we know, that doesn't qualify you as a manacoach. But how can you be passionate about growing people if you aren't wholehearted? According to Brown, the ability to be vulnerable is what all wholehearted people have in common.

If we define "wholehearted" as "having no doubt about sincerely supporting someone," can you think of any great manacoach in your life who wasn't wholehearted? When you admit to a weakness, fear, or something that you aren't proud of, that vulnerable state makes you human. Isn't the very essence of being a manacoach a desire to put others first? How can you do that if you aren't willing to be wholehearted?

## Depth

In my frequent work with management groups, I wish there was a "discomfort meter" in the room when we discuss vulnerability. I ask groups to describe issues like their most embarrassing moment, the person they have the most difficulty communicating with, their biggest fear in life, a time when they hurt someone and now regret it, or the most painful rejection they have ever suffered. With forty people in the room, the replies will range from "I am blessed in that I've never been rejected," to "not joining the family business to pursue my own dreams," to a person crying, "my father was an alcoholic and became violent when he drank."

I follow up with another go-around, asking each participant to identify the person they thought went the deepest in what they shared. No matter how large the group, everyone—and I mean everyone—agrees on one, two, or at most three out of the whole group who went the deepest. What they are really identifying are the most courageous, most powerful, or—as Brené Brown would say—the most wholehearted people in the room.

The point of this exercise is to show that being vulnerable is not easy. Our mind naturally buries those vulnerable moments in our lives. It's hard work to dig down into your subconscious and dredge up painful memories. The problem is that, if you don't develop this curiosity about yourself, you can't understand what makes you tick. If you don't know what makes you tick, how can you determine what makes those you are coaching tick?

## Why Vulnerability Is Hard Work

If you are the type of person who can't expose yourself to others by talking about something like your biggest challenge growing up or the fears that keep you awake at night, you are not alone. In fact, you are in the majority.

In my other life, I was a high school band teacher, and every two years we would take between fifty and one hundred students on tour. My colleague Daryl Wakeham, an English teacher, accompanied the group one year as a chaperone. One day, while traveling through Austria on a tour bus, Daryl walked up to the front, grabbed the microphone from the driver, and recalled the most embarrassing moments throughout his entire life. For almost an hour, he shared more than ten stories. Everyone on the bus, including the driver, was captivated by these stories, in which Daryl made fun of himself.

He then asked if anyone else wanted to come up and share their most embarrassing moments. Nobody volunteered. Even I couldn't do it . . . I was paralyzed. Not because I lacked the courage, but because I honestly couldn't think of any embarrassing moments. I knew there were thousands of them, but I couldn't bring any to mind.

Later on, I would learn that it was because my conscious mind had rammed those embarrassing moments into the depths of my subconscious mind, and I was unable to recover them. I was so frustrated with myself and so impressed with Daryl's courage that for the next three years, whenever I could think of any embarrassing experience, I would write it down and say it out loud to myself.

If you can't think of an embarrassing or challenging moment, that doesn't mean you lack courage or that you can't be vulnerable. We are brought up in a society where we are made to think that vulnerability is a weakness that will get us nowhere. In reality, it is the gateway to connecting with people who work with you. We all have a closet full of fears, insecurities, and traumatic events in our past that have hampered our development. The one thing we all hunger for is unconditional acceptance, and running the risk of being judged negatively while sharing vulnerabilities requires courage. Growth requires risk, and people on your team are more likely to take that risk if they have a manacoach who makes them feel safe. That manacoach needs to be wholehearted, and she can't be wholehearted unless she is vulnerable.

## Finding Our Vulnerabilities

For many years, whenever I learn of a client who sees a therapist he or she likes, I have booked a consult with that therapist. One such therapist was Michele Crawford. Michele teaches trauma therapy as one of her many tools. Traumatic events in our life are often buried deep inside our subconscious. If we can dig them up and deal with them, it *frees our soul.*

When I arrived, she handed me several forms where I was supposed to fill in my personal history and list the traumatic events in my life. After I completed the form, we went into a room. She dimmed the lights, put a vibrating ball in each of my hands, asked me to close my eyes, and began asking me questions. While she asked me questions about my life and we bounced around from one event to another, she used her extensive training in Eye Movement Desensitization and Reprocessing to observe the movements of my eyes under their lids.

At one point she asked me where I was, and I told her that I was in my dad's office, talking to my mom, who was in Ireland. I was attempting to tell Mom that my brother—her son—died in a car accident, and I was finding it impossible to get the words out. I was moving my mouth, but words wouldn't come out. I gave up and instead all I could say was, "Get Dad on the phone." I was barely able to speak those words.

Michele abruptly stopped the proceedings, turned on the lights, and looked through the report I wrote. She pointed out that I didn't even mention my brother Garth's death in my history where it specifically asks for traumatic events in my life.

Although Garth's death was many years behind me, it wouldn't have occurred to me consciously that this was a devastating event in my life. That session helped me to discover that the first step in self-awareness—being connected with one's self—is understanding that we can't always see ourselves clearly through our own eyes. Many of us need help in uncovering the things in our past that prevent us from moving forward.

It might be that the reason you can't be vulnerable is not because you are weak, lack courage, or are not wholehearted. Because of what you have suffered, you may have buried it so deep in your mind that you aren't able to recover it. You have to know what's behind the vulnerability before you can expose and talk about it. You have to be able to clearly see the error, weakness, embarrassing moment, or mishap for what it truly is before you can deal with it at a conscious level.

## Weakness for the Manacoach Is Hiding Weaknesses

When manacoaches admit they are wrong and ask for forgiveness, they get instant respect, the controversy is finished, and they have demonstrated true power. You can't be truly accountable if you can't own a loss, a mistake, or an accident. If a team is made up of individuals who are aware of, and responsible for, their particular accountabilities, how can the team get stronger if individuals aren't able to talk about where they are vulnerable and need help? That process starts with their manacoach, who must set the example.

The problem is that we are programmed by the culture we are from. The mainstream view is that we must not cry, because it's a sign of weakness. It's unfortunate that from a young age, we are taught that if we want to influence others and gain respect from others, we must never show weakness.

Just the other day, I was working with a management team, and one of the team members said, "This is all well and good, but in business, showing weakness can leave you bankrupt. When you are in front of people you are manacoaching, they expect you to have answers, not questions. They expect you to be strong and confident, not weak and sobbing."

If you agree with that statement, you are not alone. In fact, you are in the majority. But instead of collecting data or discussing reams of research and theory, I want to put you in the shoes of a director who sits on the board of two different companies.

*Company A* has a CEO whose name is Jill, and this morning at your board meeting, she reports a complete screw-up in her management of the company. The mistake is expensive, and it will take time and a lot of money for the company to recover. You ask Jill who is to blame for this mistake. Her response is simple: "I am." Fighting back tears, she goes on to say that it was her idea, it occurred on her watch, and she takes full responsibility. She explains where the flaws were in her thinking, and she now has a plan and procedures in place to make sure it never happens again. She throws herself on the wisdom of the board and completely understands if they can't offer the forgiveness she is requesting.

In *Company B*, Jack is the CEO reporting to you and the rest of the board. This company has had a similar meltdown. But Jack assures you all that it wasn't his fault. You thought Jack was proud and strong, but you have to listen to Jack ramble on about how the CFO needs to be terminated, and he goes on to list all the other people who were responsible. Jack even has a cute, well-prepared response when you ask how he will ensure that this won't happen again. But something just doesn't seem right, and "authentic" and "accountable" are not the words that are coming to your mind.

I have no data to throw at you, no special circumstances to convince you that one CEO is better than the other. Some might say that Jill was weak, as she didn't have the strength to defend herself. She just took full responsibility for the error. She had no excuses.

She is transparent and has opened herself up for criticism, ridicule, and being fired. But go deep in your soul and ask yourself this: as a director, who do you want running your company? What is your stomach telling you about Jack versus Jill? Which CEO impresses you at the moment? And the critical question is this: *Who would you want watching your back if you had to choose a team to perform with?*

We don't need to know the details of the meltdown in either of the companies to answer those questions. We don't need to know Jack and Jill's beliefs, skill sets, or personalities to answer those questions. Some would still say that you can't show vulnerability like Jill. Manacoaches know differently. Manacoaches know that they not only set the example—they are the example. They have to be less concerned with people listening to them and more concerned with team members *watching* them. A good manacoach knows the power of vulnerability. Admitting that nobody is perfect starts with them. If they aren't willing to be vulnerable, nobody else will.

## *Saying* You're Sorry versus *Asking* for Forgiveness

When I worked as a manager in charge of sales some years ago, my son Jamie was ten years old. We had just bought expensive leather furniture for the living room, and I set a rule: no more eating in the living room. A few days later, I got home late from a baseball game, made a sandwich, grabbed a drink, and headed for the living room to watch the recap of the game on TV. Jamie wakes up, comes downstairs to get a drink of water, and asks me why I'm breaking the rule of no eating in the living room. I have a few choices in responding:

1. I can ignore him and tell him to get his water and get back to bed.

2.    I can tell him that because I'm the head honcho of the family and I bring home the bacon, I'm allowed to break the rule every once in a while.

3.    I can take full responsibility by saying, "Jamie, you are right, and my behavior here is doubly wrong. I was the one who set the rule, and then I broke it. Can you forgive me?"

Now, make no mistake. Jamie's emotional state will not be affected by which option I choose. But depending on which response I choose, a lesson will be delivered and received. If I choose the first or second response, Jamie won't be upset. But he will be thinking about the lesson he has just learned, which is that when you get to the top, you don't have to be accountable, and the rules that you enforce on others don't apply to you.

But here is the great thing about a response like the third one. Owning up stops everything negative. It stops the controversy in its tracks. It stops background noise. It stops the talking behind others' backs. It stops the politics and allows everyone to move on.

In addition, saying "I'm sorry" admits that you have made a mistake, but it doesn't ask for a response. It doesn't determine whether or not you have been forgiven. Vulnerability takes strength and so does asking for forgiveness. Asking for forgiveness is a question, while saying you are sorry is merely a statement (thank you for that lesson, the Honorable David Sweet!). The next time you feel you need to apologize to someone, instead of just saying "I'm sorry," include the question, "Can you forgive me?" It's amazing how something so simple is so difficult to ask.

Do you have a person in your life who says he or she is sorry so often that you just roll your eyes? When you say you are sorry, you have only acknowledged what you are sorry about; you haven't determined the response. You can't demand to be forgiven. You haven't reestablished trust, which is the basis for moving forward with that person. Saying that you are sorry is a nice gesture, and it acknowledges a mistake. But real courage is required to ask for forgiveness, simply because it requires you to surrender to another's will. The answer might be *no*. And if it is, the issues around that negative response must be dealt with, or the relationship will not move forward—it will move backward, begin disintegrating, or even cease to exist.

In a former corporate job, I worked with a marketing manager who hid from her team in her office. She had many weaknesses, both in marketing and in dealing with people, and she would have been so much easier to work with if she exposed those weaknesses to both her team and me and asked for help. On one occasion, she was responsible for a mistake in printing a mass run of brochures that cost the company over a million dollars.

I honestly don't know if we could have forgiven her had she come out of her office, sat down with us, acknowledged the mistake, and asked for forgiveness. But she didn't. Instead she hid in her office, behind her keyboard, and through e-mails tried to blame the printing company, the designers, and even individuals on her team.

"The buck stops here." Harry Truman had the quote engraved on a plaque on his desk, and John Kennedy said it in reference to the Bay of Pigs fiasco in Cuba. There is no better phrase to explain "accountability," and the opposite in "passing the buck" is not being accountable. The courage required in calling yourself out, admitting a mistake, and asking for forgiveness is tremendous, yet regardless of how it turns out, you gain the respect of everyone on your team by taking full accountability.

## If You Can't Be Vulnerable, Don't Manage People

If you manage people and get absolutely nothing from watching Brené Brown's videos, then I beg you to leave your position. If you aren't currently managing people, please don't consider it until you do the work to discover yourself and your own vulnerabilities.

Instead, apply your talents where both you and the people around you will benefit. In *The Storyteller's Secret*, Carmine Gallo does a great job of defining "passion." It's what makes your heart sing. I like to golf, but it's not my passion. Gallo gives the example of Rory McIlroy: the last thing he thinks about before going to sleep at night and the first thing he thinks about when waking up is golf. That is Rory's passion. My passion is disrupting the way people think.

The manacoach's passion has to be growing people. You can't grow people if you can't connect with them, and you can't connect with anyone if you don't feel worthy. And according to Brené Brown, you can't feel worthy of connection unless you are wholehearted. Wholehearted manacoaches have that magical, critical ingredient called "vulnerability." I'm sorry to say, it's not enough to love people. Your number-one role as a manacoach is the constant attention to removing barriers for your team members. To do that you have to be able to connect, and that is impossible unless you are willing to be vulnerable. Vulnerability is the common denominator in all tried-and-true manacoaches.

# CHAPTER 6 FOLLOW-UP

1.  Identify how many embarrassing moments you can recall in your lifetime. If it's only a couple, even though there are hundreds, you are normal. When they come to mind from this point forward write them down.

2.  The next time you find yourself apologizing, make a conscious effort to ask for forgiveness. See if you can feel the vulnerability and how much more difficult it is to ask than just saying you are sorry.

3.  The next time someone makes a stupid mistake or has an embarrassing mishap, sit down with them and describe when something similar happened to you. Feel the connection that takes place.

If you think these three exercises are pointless, then do the world a favor and don't manage people until you change your perspective.

# Manacoach #1 Role: Remove Barriers

Vulnerability   *Path to remove barriers*

↑

Whole Hearted   *Love = Unconditional*
*acceptance of me and you*

↑

Awareness   *Of me and my surroundings*

↑

Curiousness   *Kills assumptions*
*and arrogance*

## chapter 7

# THE MANACOACH ON HIRING

> *"My recruiting key—I looked for people first, athletes second. I wanted people with a sound value system, as you cannot buy values. You're only as good as your values. I learned early on that you do not put greatness into people . . . but somehow try to pull it out."*

## —HERB BROOKS

*This is a true story. The names have been changed to protect the innocent.*

Jack is desperate to hire a bookkeeper. He is a people person who doesn't realize that the biggest mistake managers make is hiring people they like personally. Jack doesn't realize yet that the person he needs is a process-oriented person, which is someone who won't warm up to him right away. Jack dismisses the first person because he is not easy to communicate with—he likes people who are more boisterous. He hits it off with the second applicant. Jack talks to her for an hour. He thinks Jill has all the right answers, although Jack is not up to speed in accounting and hasn't written out questions or prepared any competency tests.

Jack feels really good about Jill, and that's a good thing because Jack cherishes his gut feeling. He contacts one reference and can't get through, and then the reference won't return his call. Jack hires Jill solely based on his gut feeling.

Six months later, Jack's accountant audits the books and tells Jack that Jill is incompetent. He is strongly advised to dismiss Jill and have certified accountants come in (for tens of thousands of dollars) to put the billing back in line. Jack is back in the same place he started, but he has now unnecessarily exposed the assets of the corporation by hiring Jill, whose failure to make timely filings cost the organization over $50,000. All of this was the result of a bad hire.

For manacoaches, great performance must be based on great processes. They know that it's critical to follow a proven process for hiring. If no one is following a proven hiring process, then bad hires are going to happen a lot.

Tony Hsieh, CEO of Zappos, says that bad hires have cost him over $100 million. In a survey, a full 27 percent of people who hire staff said that a bad hire costs at least $50,000. Others who were surveyed said a bad hire can cost as much as two and a half times the person's salary. We could quote all sorts of numbers from thousands of studies to make the point that a bad hire disrupts the company's work flow, productivity, finances, and reputation. The manacoach should execute some simple, systematic procedures not to just avoid making a bad hire but also to hire the right person—the A Player, the person the competition would die for. The manacoach ensures that this person is being put in a position where his or her talents will be well utilized.

## The Ideal Candidate

There are three factors to look at in hiring the right person. The manacoach needs to ensure that she is hiring the right person, that she is putting that person in the right position, and that the person she is hiring can competently and efficiently bring tasks to completion. Let's make this as simple as possible: the right person is the one who fits the core values of the organization. Are the candidate's values in line with the people he or she is going to be working with? Leading-edge companies make certain that they are not just posting their core values on some fancy plaque in the reception area but are hiring, firing, rewarding, and recognizing based on their stated core values.

For example, EOS Worldwide has hundreds of professionally trained and certified implementers across the world, helping entrepreneurial business owners get more out of their business by implementing a proven management operating system. EOS's core values are taken off the wall and entrenched in the culture. It's important to have a "story" that explains your core value statements. The story can be short with bullet points, it can be longer with examples of behaviors that align with the core values, or you can use analogies to crystalize what these statements actually mean. If anyone is not aligned with their core values, then they simply don't get hired or certified. Here are the core values that define the culture at EOS Worldwide:

1.   **Be humbly confident.** Story: Open, honest, real, well-practiced, ready to make a positive difference

2.   **Grow or die.** Story: Driven to maximize every situation and to take ourselves and our clients to the next level

3.  **Help first.** Story: Subordinating our personal interests to advance others and always giving value before expecting anything in return

4.  **Do the right thing.** Story: Never betraying a trust and doing whatever it takes to resolve every issue so people can move forward

5.  **Do what you say.** Story: Sometimes more, never less

Two of these core value statements really resonate with me. They have existed in every one of my careers, which means they are paramount to me in terms of resonating with who I am.

At EOS Worldwide, "Help first" means that you are willing, able, and eager to help everyone. Even though the implementers are competing against each other for clients, they help each other out in terms of giving advice and support. Mike Paton, coauthor of *Get a Grip*, is a busy man. He's a Certified EOS Implementer, sought-after speaker, and the visionary of EOS Worldwide, responsible (among other things) for training new professional EOS Implementers and running the Quarterly Collaborative Exchanges for the worldwide EOS Implementer Community. Yet he still finds time to help his colleagues out at every request. Not helping your colleagues is completely acceptable in some cultures, because you are competing against them, and you don't get paid for it. Within the EOS Implementer Community, if you don't believe in helping others, including your colleagues, you will not fit the culture and are not the right person for the job. You will not survive in the organization.

"Grow or die" means that you are either growing or dying within the organization. If you work at EOS, you must constantly be upgrading your skills and investing in yourself, because EOS's clients rely on their implementer to be in a constant state of growth and improvement. To avoid becoming redundant, each implementer must keep ahead of the industry.

Some people are confused by "core values" and "attitude." The way we behave is determined by the way we think. An "attitude" is just the way a person thinks. Some people are considered positive and others negative. Some have a friendly attitude, and some don't. Some are optimistic, and some are pessimistic. People choose their attitudes, and the manacoach understands a critically important rule: *you can't change another person's attitude—you can only change your own.* Unfortunately, the closer a person is to us or the more we want someone in our lives, the more we try to break this rule. Manacoaches know that they can't change an attitude; they can only create an environment where change is possible through the courage to initiate open and honest dialogue. When the manacoach thinks a coworker's behavior (behavior determined by attitude) is not in line with a specific core value (what the company believes to be right, true, and good), she "enters the danger zone" in discussing her observations with specific examples.

## Measuring the Alignment of Core Values

As previously mentioned in chapter 5, a simple way to define a culture is by its core values. These can be identified by looking at what you believe to be true about the people you work with. What are the three to seven words or statements that could encapsulate your culture?

Perhaps one of your core values would be to "tell the truth no matter what." Now you might be asking, who wouldn't have this as a value? We put the following scenario in front of eight business owners: a customer is considering placing a large order with you and needs it delivered in three months. You realize that you can't produce enough material in that time frame to meet the order. Do you tell the truth and run the risk of your customer going somewhere else, or do you make the commitment, even though you know you will be asking for forgiveness in the future?

Four of the eight business owners we interviewed would tell the truth, and four of them would take the order and work things out later on. All eight business owners are good people who run healthy businesses, but four of them did not have a core value of "brutal honesty no matter what." This is not a question of ethics . . . it just is.

As a manacoach, if your company has not identified the core values that everyone operates in line with, then you have to do your best to identify them. The reason for this is that you need to develop interview questions and other types of evaluation tools to measure a new hire's alignment with these core values.

My dad was always big on good manners and respecting everyone in his workplace. When I was older, I was able to identify these as a few of his core values. He would never hire someone unless he had the opportunity to take that person out to a restaurant. The applicant most likely wasn't aware that my dad was observing how he or she interacted with the host and service staff. An applicant wouldn't be hired if he or she failed to treat the service staff with good manners and the utmost respect. Regardless of their status, treating everyone with respect was a core value that my dad cherished.

Manacoaches go over the core values of the organization. They tell the story behind each one and give examples of both how they do and do not work in practice. The more the applicant understands about your culture, the more you both can determine whether that person fits within the organization.

Be careful that you are being totally honest about your core values. Jim Collins talks about "aspirational" core values. Are they really aligned with everyone in the organization, or do you simply wish they were?

Let's say you run a hospital, and you would like a core value to be "treating patients with respect and courtesy." However, some of your best doctors have no bedside abilities at all. Are you prepared to let them go? If not, you have to be brutally honest with how important that core value is to you and to the success of the organization.

## Linking the Right Person to the Right Job

Once the right person for the organization has been determined, the next step is to determine if that person meets the requirements of the job. Jim Collins first created the concept of having the "right person" in the "right seat" in his book *Good to Great*, and since then his idea has been used by many. The late Bill Bonnstetter, an expert on behavior assessments and founder of Target Training in Arizona, famously said, "If the job could talk, what would it say it needs?"

The manacoach examines the job to determine all its key roles and functions, then determines the competencies and skill sets required to be successful in the position. For example, most positions in sales demand an extroverted, people-oriented person, while most accountant positions demand an introverted, process-oriented person who is passionate about detail and precision.

There are three ways we can evaluate how qualified people are at doing their job, or their "seat":

1.  We can ask them about it in the interview and test them on the necessary skills to do the job.

2.  We can ask their references or people they have worked for in the past.

3.    We can get a professional to evaluate the person through behavior assessments and personality tests.

During the interview stage, we can ask questions formulated by an expert in the field to see if the candidate has the experience and attributes we are looking for. If we were hiring a bookkeeper, we would administer a short test during the interview process to see if the applicant has the required competencies that have been previously identified. For example, how is a balance sheet structured? Or explain the following: the payroll taxes were overdeposited by $35.00 and a refund check was received for the overdeposit. The check was deposited in the bank and credited to miscellaneous income. What do you do?

If we are hiring a salesperson, a great approach is to have them prepare a presentation to try and "sell us" on a product that they sold in the past.

If you are thinking that you could overkill this part of the process, then think back to the beginning of the chapter, on the cost of a bad hire. The manacoach wants the A players. She wants to leave the B and C players for the competition. Research the right questions, and don't hesitate to err on the side of too many skill tests that are directly related to the job.

## Reference Checks

Reference checks are becoming more difficult to obtain due to liability concerns, but don't let this deter you from trying. Gleaning useful information from a reference is also a bit of an art form, in that you need to listen to what is *not* being said more than what *is* being said about your candidate. One question that must always be asked of the reference is, "If you had a position open, would you hire this person back?"

You are not listening for a *yes*. You are listening for hesitation, something like, "Ahhh . . . well, we don't have a position to hire [him/her] back." They might even respond with, "Ahhh . . . that's a good question." It is a good question, and if they hesitate in answering it, they have given you the answer—*no*.

Let's consider this powerful single question for a second. Think of a person you loved to work with in the past. This is a person you miss working with immensely. If I were to ask you if you would hire that person back or work with that person again, here are some of the responses I would get from you without any hesitation: "You bet, in a second," "Sure, he was great," or "To tell you the truth, we have a position open, and if you don't hire him, we will."

When you do reference checks, see if you can find out about other managers, departments, or companies the applicant worked for, and follow up on those. The future cost of a bad hire is on your shoulders if you ignore the signals that your applicant has a questionable past.

The manacoach may have an HR department to assist in hiring, but you must not abdicate the hiring process to them. They can assist you, but as the manacoach, you must be involved in the process and have the last say because in the right type of company, you will be held responsible for the applicant's performance.

## Behavior Assessments

The next phase in hiring is assessing behavior styles. A number of very good assessments will give you reliable predictions on how the person communicates, behaves, and interacts with other people and information. Target Training, Myers-Briggs, Kolbe, and others will help you place the right person in the right seat. These assessments will tell you in minutes what would normally take you six months to learn about a person.

As you research the best tools, you will find that everyone has their favorite assessment, and they swear by it. Patrick Lencioni and his company endorse Myers-Briggs. Marcus Buckingham endorses Strengths Finder. Gino Wickman and EOS Worldwide endorse Kolbe. Tony Robbins endorses DISC, from Target Training International. All the assessments have their differences, but all in all, it's been our experience that each is not much different than your smartphone—they are all good, but most people prefer to stick with the one they started with. Those who started with the iPhone stick with it, and those who start with Samsung do the same.

## How Do These Assessments Work?

Behavior assessments are based on years of observation by psychologists who have been able to predict people's behavior styles by how they respond to various instruments. Most assessments use quadrants represented by initials, colors, or words. Depending on how people respond, you can make reliable predictions about their preferences for interacting with people, their way of thinking through problems, and their communication styles.

If you put a hundred people in a room, you could divide them into two groups: those who are predominantly introverts and those who are extroverts. You could then split each of those two groups into those who are predominantly people-oriented and those who are process-oriented or results-oriented. We say *predominantly* because only a very small percentage of people fit in only one quadrant.

Depending on the person's dominant quadrant, the assessment is able to make predictions. For example, extroverted, process-oriented people tend to be determined, forceful, direct, and very competitive. They make quick decisions, and they can appear to be angry when they are stressed or frustrated. Don't tell them how to do something; just tell them what needs to be done. After that, just stand back and let them go. Kolbe calls this person a high "quick start," Myers-Briggs calls this person "ESTP," Target Training Institute calls this person a "high D," and Color Code would label the same person "red." Most people stick to the assessment test they learned so they don't have to relearn the different labels and language that, with small modifications, mean the same thing.

Our company has been using behavior assessments over the past sixteen years, and we have been able to determine that extroverted people-oriented individuals make good salespeople. This is not to say that introverts are not good at sales, for there are many exceptions to prove this. This is why you should not make hiring decisions based solely on these types of assessments. Any good book on hiring will support this.

## Giving the Green Light to Proceed

It's heavily recommended that the manacoach get two out of three green lights before hiring a candidate. For example, you have an impressive interview with a candidate, the candidate does well on all the skills tests, and the candidate seems to be in line with all the core values—that is one green light. If you conduct a thorough reference check and everyone's response is, "The candidate is a rock star at the job," then that is another green light. The third green light can be found through whatever behavior assessments you use.

Imagine you are hiring a salesperson. From the interview, you find that she is in line with your core values and has a great attitude. From your testing, you know that she understands your systems and knows the selling process well. That's one green light. Every reference you checked with states in no uncertain terms and without hesitation that she can do a great job. That is another green light. Unfortunately, the advisor who provides you with the behavior assessments says that she is an introverted, process-oriented person and will be stressed by the job. That would be a red light.

You have two out of three green lights, so it's okay to go ahead and hire her. You can use the behavior assessment to identify what to watch out for, so all is not lost. It's always nice to have three green lights, and even though good assessments are very reliable, they still aren't 100 percent accurate. In a few situations, we have found candidates who did not get a green light on the assessment but turned out to be exceptional in their role.

Imagine yourself as a baseball coach. If you were interviewing someone for a catcher position, wouldn't you test him to see if he could consistently throw the ball to second base without any effort (a critical skill set for the position of catcher in baseball)? Would you check his performance records from other teams (reference checks) to ensure that he could do the job? Would you do whatever assessments were required to make sure that he could communicate with the pitcher and other team members well and that he didn't have anger issues?

The reality is, if the manacoach makes a bad hire, it ends up costing the organization a lot of money. It distracts everyone from the business at hand.

I become extremely anxious when I hear a manacoach trying to create or modify a job for a specific person. The other day, I was party to a business owner trying to redefine a function for his son. This meant that I was getting paid an insane amount of money to tell this guy that his son needed to go and find a job where his talents could be better utilized. Creating jobs or functions to suit a person is a kind of denial, and it rarely works. What would the job or function say it needs (if it could talk), and who is the person with the best skills and talent to do the job?

If you correctly identify what job skills are needed, you interview and test to make sure the person who wants the job can meet those needs, you find that the person's attitude and core values are in line with the company's expectations, there's been a successful reference check completed, and the person has the aptitude and behavior style that fits the job, the chances are far in your favor that there will be no regrets. Of course there are no promises, but the plane is significantly less likely to crash if *all* the boxes are checked before it takes off.

We promise.

# CHAPTER 7 FOLLOW-UP

1.   Be sure a professional looks at the wording in your ad placements, publications, and wherever else you are posting the job. The wording and placement is paramount.

2.   When you go through the resumes, make sure you get back to the applicant in a very timely manner.

3.   Interview with a second person in the room designated to ask the documented questions while you observe.

4.   Have an off-site activity where you get to see the applicant interact with people.

5.   Review the applicant's behavior style and make sure it fits the job in question.

6.   Have a leave-behind folder that includes testimonials from your staff and the benefits you offer. "Sell" the prospect on why you are a great place to work.

7.   Don't make the applicant wait if you have an offer to present. "A" players have lots of offers to choose from.

## chapter 8

# THE MANACOACH ON FIRING

> *"Firing someone is not necessarily a sign of accountability but is often the last act of cowardice."*
>
> **—PATRICK LENCIONI, *THE ADVANTAGE***

Leaders identify the direction, and the manacoach ensures her team implements and executes what is required to get there. I once asked Marcus Buckingham, who has done extensive research and identified many reasons behind poor performance, what he considered to be the most significant factor in not getting there. He didn't hesitate for a second: "Unclear expectations from management."

If you fire an employee and that employee is shocked or upset, then there is a pretty good chance that you are the one who should be fired, and you should be thoroughly ashamed of yourself. Not only have you failed but you have unintentionally hurt someone with a sucker punch. I hear stories where someone gets fired by text or email, by an HR person when their manager didn't have the guts to show up, or the person had absolutely no idea she was about to lose her job, and it makes me want to come out of my skin. Why?

As a manacoach, you have the livelihood of people and their families in your hands. It is a huge responsibility, and unfortunately in business, there are far too many cowards who have no business being in this position of immense responsibility. As a manacoach, you have a tough job—a job that requires immense courage, especially when addressing people face-to-face. You need to have the guts to let team members know where they stand and whether or not they are meeting critical expectations. If you aren't empathetic and don't care about your team members, then as Tom Peters has been saying for over three decades, "Don't go out and ruin another company. Do everyone a favor and don't be a manager."

In the movie *Miracle*, when Herb Brooks (Kurt Russell) cuts the last player, Ralph Cox, before leaving for the Olympics in 1980, it shows Herb calm and collected in his office as he delivers the bad news. This is not what actually happened. Today, Ralph Cox will tell you that he was called to Herb's hotel room at the team's Olympic send-off banquet in Minnesota. According to Cox, he was summoned to Herb's hotel room, and when he went in, Herb was pacing about, visibly stressed and shaken. He was probably gathering the courage to have a really difficult conversation to cut Cox. Cox was the right person but didn't have the skill level to go to the Olympics with the team. When I tell this story to audiences, I get emotional, especially when I tell them what Herb said years later when asked what he was thinking about when his team stood on the podium receiving their gold medals. He said he was thinking about Ralph Cox and what a great guy he was. Being a manacoach requires the courage to let people know where they stand face-to-face—no excuses.

In 1998, Patrick Lencioni published a book titled *The Five Temptations of a CEO*, and the second temptation that he identified is "accountability"—more specifically, creating a culture of accountability by making sure that your expectations are clearly communicated and met. Patrick concluded that if you are able to avoid the temptation to not have critical conversations with your team members, then rarely should you ever have to fire anyone. (A "critical conversation" is what we call a dialogue where the manacoach reviews one or more critical expectations that are not being met. "Critical" means the employee will not be in his or her job if the expectation is not met in a defined time line.) Patrick said that when these critical conversations take place, close to 85 percent of the time, the employee will either meet the expectation or leave of his or her own accord. But based on my observations over the past fifteen years, this percentage is actually higher. Firing is not necessary.

We naturally want and deserve to know where we stand in a relationship. It's important that we know if we are meeting expectations, because if we are not—and if this shortcoming is brought to our attention in a clear and concise manner—we can act accordingly and choose our response. But as team members, if we aren't meeting expectations, and our manager doesn't have the courage and decency to communicate that to us, then how can we adjust and be successful?

And by the way, Ralph Cox knew why he was being summoned to Herb Brooks's hotel room before he arrived—no doubt in his mind.

I'm often asked, "How often should I communicate expectations?" There is no singular answer, but you can follow a general rule of thumb. Your team members should know whether they are meeting expectations. That should occur on at least a quarterly basis. If someone is not meeting expectations, you must have the courage to talk to the team member and write a follow-up letter that clarifies your points.

I often will sit down with a business owner or CEO to help address a performance issue with a certain team member. My first question is always, "Does the employee know what is expected of her?" Usually they will say yes. I expect that response, so I then make a request that catches many of them off guard: "Show me." Don't tell me about the expectation that is not being met; show me the document that you have both read that outlines the critical expectations that aren't being met. I learned a rule a long time ago from Jim Renahan: if it's not in writing, it doesn't exist. As a manacoach, if you haven't communicated your expectations in writing, then it cannot be assumed that your team member understands what those expectations are.

Let's be clear. We are not talking about a manual, or a five-page job description, or a twenty-page performance review form. You should identify the ten to twenty things that you expect of that position and highlight the five to seven critical expectations that must be met or the team members are let go. It's unfortunate to say, but if you did this, to refer back to the previous discussion on critical conversations, you would be ahead of more than 85 percent of your peers. As a manacoach, it is common to have a difficult time knowing exactly what the problem is regarding a performance issue. Something that a team member is doing does not sit right with us, but we can't really identify the specifics, so it's difficult to begin the conversation. If this is the case, then draw a triangle. At one corner, write "Attitude/Values." At the next, write "Performance," and at the third corner, write "Ability to Complete."

## Attitude/Values

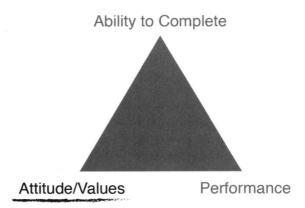

Jack the manacoach is stumped. His top salesperson, Superduper, constantly outsells his three teammates combined. Month in and month out, Superduper always lands the majority of the deals. The problem is that Superduper is rude. He's rude to clients when the deal is not going his way. He's rude to the service technicians when he thinks they aren't moving fast enough on his accounts. He's disrespectful to the front-line people if he feels things aren't moving fast enough. Superduper is constantly late for meetings, and when he does show up, the spotlight has to be on him or he huffs and puffs and constantly interrupts. Superduper also lies to customers and teammates all the time. Never mind working with Superduper; nobody in the organization likes being in his vicinity. Jack doesn't want to lose his top salesperson, but neither does he want to lose most of the people on his staff who hate working with Superduper.

A lot has been written about soft skills and hard skills. Let's keep it as simple as possible by accepting that attitude (the way we think), and values (what we believe to be right, true, and good) are "soft skills," or the soft side of a person. I love challenging an audience with the question "What is an attitude?" Although many of us use the word often, we don't consider its meaning. Attitude is the way we think. If we think negatively, then we have a negative attitude. If we think positively, we have a positive attitude. If we are always happy, we have a happy attitude, and if we go with the flow, we have an easygoing attitude. Yet none of these are constant; we fluctuate between different attitudes depending on our mood. It's no wonder that attitudes are so difficult to manage, because they can change by the minute depending on a person's reaction or understanding of something. It's easy to understand why it's difficult to apply raw measurements to attitude and values. This is why we call them "soft skills."

Some of us are wired to understand people, some are wired to understand numbers, and some are wired to understand strategy. Certain people enjoy meeting people, and others would prefer to avoid them. Some love evaluating theories or balancing numbers, and some don't. Some are optimistic, and some are pessimistic. It all depends on their attitude. But every manacoach knows that *it is impossible to change someone else's attitude or the way they think.*

It is your responsibility as a manacoach to point out what parts of a person's attitude are acceptable and not acceptable; however, the only one who can change an attitude is the person in question. And here is the kicker: the closer someone is to us in any relationship, or the more important they are as a player on the team, the more we want to ignore the fact that we can't change the way another person thinks. *We can't change their attitude.* We can only bring the issue(s) to their attention and make our expectations clear.

To address a soft-skill issue, write down all those things that are important to you and the success of your team in terms of how a person should behave. This might include descriptors like respectful, kind, positive, helpful, generous, can-do, watches the other person's back, trustworthy, honest, competitive, reliable, and many others. Now write out what is important to you and your team members in terms of what you expect. Refer to the organization's core values if they are truly understood and followed. The more clarity you can bring to your expectations, the better the results. After you do this, determine what would be nice to see versus what is critical.

For example, I personally feel that respect is hugely important. My expectation for people I work with, whether I'm reporting to them or they are reporting to me, is that they be respectful. It's true that you can't polish rocks without friction, so conflict is a necessary part of growth. But to maintain a healthy relationship, we must maintain respect for each other during the conflict. Don't attack people's dignity or who they are. I don't care how good you are at what you do or how much I need you. If you aren't respectful, then I don't want to be associated with you.

So if I am Jack, I identify how Superduper is not meeting my expectations with regard to respect. I should have at least three specific examples (the more the better) of this type of unacceptable behavior. I write a letter clearly defining a critical expectation (one that must be met or else, at some defined point, the relationship will come to an end). I cite the specific examples of concern, and the last paragraph should always end with: "If this isn't clear, or you have any questions or concerns, please get back to me by Friday, or I will take your silence as acceptance and clear understanding of these expectations." Never deliver the letter before the conversation, but it's a good idea to write it out beforehand for added clarity while you're talking. After the conversation, deliver the letter personally, and explain that it's just a review of the discussion.

Delivering the letter to the team member is the most difficult part of the process. If I had a nickel for every manacoach who had the talk but didn't deliver the letter out of fear, I'd be rich.

Jack cannot change Bill's attitude, but as a manacoach, it is his key responsibility to let Bill know that his attitude is neither acceptable nor sustainable in the culture. Now Bill is clear on the state of things, and he has a choice either to reevaluate and adjust his attitude or to look for another job.

Many manacoaches ask, "What is the time line? And how often do we have to communicate these concerns before letting the team member go?" There is no tried-and-true answer. This is the manacoach's call, and it's based on a number of factors. It will be determined by the answers to questions like, "How serious is it in terms of cost and damage being created?" "How long has the team member been with you?" "How difficult is it to replace the team member, and are they in the middle of a project?" The consultant who has a "one-size-fits-all" answer to the question of when to let a person go doesn't understand the question. However, you must have a plan in mind as to what the time frame is and how many times you are going to give a team member a chance to improve (at least three is the general rule). If you don't know, then the team member certainly doesn't, and that is just not right.

Again, just because something is simple doesn't mean it's easy. Relationships, whether they are with spouses, family, church groups, sports teams, musical ensembles, dance groups, or business units, require critical expectations to be communicated and acted on when they aren't being met. It requires courage and follow-up, and if you don't have those, you will never be a manacoach.

## Performance

Ability to Complete

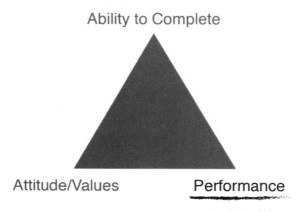

Attitude/Values          Performance

Joyful has a solid attitude. She fits the core values of the organization and demonstrates great character. You can trust her to watch your back, and she is always there when you need her. The problem is that Joyful has performance issues. She can't keep up with the needs of her role in the warehouse. In the past few years the company has grown, and to keep up with the growth, it has brought automation and technology to many of the processes that Joyful is responsible for. Jane is her manacoach, and she is stressed because there is no other role for Joyful in the organization, but Joyful is such a likable person that Jane is stalling in addressing these issues with her.

Jane is stalling to deal with this for a good reason. The toughest thing for a manacoach to do is to cut players like Ralph Cox, who are great people but can't keep up with the requirements of the job. Business is a performance activity. The better your people perform, the more points you score. When we know that an employee can't do the job, can we be compassionate while also holding that employee accountable?

As we've said, it's good to know exactly what the problem is before discussing performance problems with a team member. I thank Gino

Wickman, author of *Traction* and founder of EOS Worldwide, from whom I got the acronym "GWC." It represents three questions: Does Joyful get it? Does she want it? Does she have the capacity to do it?

**Gets it.** To "get" your job means that you are genetically wired for it—you were born to do that job. Think of a server in a restaurant who takes your table's order, and just before she puts the order in, she glances at your table from forty feet across the room. She can tell by your facial expression and table gestures if you have changed your mind, and she'll immediately return to ask if everything is okay. This server is a perfect example of someone who just "gets" it.

You can't teach this, you can't train for it, you can't send someone to school for it, you can't coach it, and you can't manage it. They either get it, or they don't. However, the manacoach must bring it to the team member's attention when analyzing his performance. "I don't think you get your job, and here's why." The manacoach provides at least three specific examples. Staying with the example of the server, say you have one who walks by tables without looking at the customers for cues. You see guests attempting to get the server's attention, but she is unable to pick up on it. Good servers are always keeping an eye on their tables to watch for signs of opportunities to assist.

You can't teach or train "getting it," but if your server doesn't instinctively know that she needs to be paying attention and scanning for signs of customer needs *all of the time*, you owe it to that server to sit down and talk about this skill. To prevent any arguments, you need to give the server at least three specific examples—with dates, times, and exact situations—where that server missed important customer cues. It's unlikely that you will see a change, but it does happen. More importantly, as a manacoach, you owe your team members a chance to correct their mistakes.

**Wants it.** When I taught high school, we had a great basketball program. Jared, the head basketball coach, used to go to the neighboring elementary schools during off-season and look for twelve-year-olds with big feet. In our district, it was a generally accepted assumption that if you had big feet in grade five, you were instantly recruited for basketball. It didn't matter if you were interested in the game, if you were only three feet tall, how athletic you were, or even whether or not you could throw a ball. Jared would make sure that those twelve-year-olds with size thirteen-plus feet made it out for all the regular basketball practices, because Jared knew that they were going to be extremely tall by the time they were on the senior team. Fast-forward six years, and Jared would usually have a star center who was over six-foot-seven and playing extremely well. His star player "got" the game, and there was no problem with "capacity."

It's easy to identify Jared's worst nightmare in this situation. Jared's star player, who he recruited seven years ago, doesn't "want" to play the game anymore. Nothing can be more frustrating for Jared, the manacoach, than to have a star player that was born to do the job and just oozes talent (gets it) and is able to learn a new trick every day (has the capacity) but doesn't *want* to do the job. If you ever suspect that one of your team members doesn't want the job, then initiate a conversation with them. Start with, "I get the impression you don't really want to be here," or "I get the impression you don't really like what you do." If an employee is working only because she needs the money or because a friend or family member wants her to have a job, the answer is clear. She doesn't want to be doing your team's work.

I went out with friends to a nice restaurant where the waiter introduced himself. I asked him if he liked his job. He responded by saying that he wanted to be a radio announcer in New York, but he didn't get the job so he "ended up being a waiter." Needless to say, he didn't want to be our waiter, and as it turned out, we didn't want him to be our waiter either, and we let the restaurant know it.

Think about the chores your parents used to make you do. My dad made me cut the lawn. I hated it. I procrastinated. I fell behind so it would grow too long. I did an overall terrible job. If I was an employee instead of a family member, I would have been fired. I got it, and I had the capacity, but I didn't want to do it. It was misery for both me and my dad. When a team member doesn't want to be doing his or her job, performance will always suffer, and so will the team's results. Jimmy Pattison, a well-known Canadian billionaire, ended his biography *Jimmy* with three words: "You gotta wanna!"

**Capacity** is teachable. If I ask you what two plus two is and you say three, obviously we have a problem. So I sit down with you or send you to a training course, and you are taught that when we add two things to two things, we have four things. If, upon your return, I ask you again what two plus two is and you say three, we have a capacity issue.

Capacity issues can be determined by asking this question: "Can the team member perform the necessary tasks to do the job *effectively* and *efficiently*?" If the answer is no, then the question becomes "Can they learn how to do it properly?"

Our ideal server in the restaurant might get the job and want the job, but let's say the restaurant is part of a national chain and introduces a new technology for tracking transactions, and the server isn't able to learn how to operate it. You would have a capacity issue. If you can't work out a solution where the server is being supported in some way to bypass this new requirement, she doesn't have the capacity to do the job, and as a manacoach, you must act accordingly.

On a side note, we've always believed that you do not have an obligation to address a capacity problem in someone who has just started. If a new team member assured you that he or she could do the job and had all the skill sets, you have no obligation to train that new member. However, if you asked a current team member to shift roles, then your organization definitely has an obligation to train if there is a capacity issue. This only makes sense.

This takes us back to the story of Herb Brooks and Ralph Cox. There is nothing worse than having to let someone go because of performance issues when that individual has a great attitude and brings every characteristic and value that you hold dear. It's not a team member's fault that she may not get it, want it, and/or have the capacity to do it. Once the manacoach finds out, though, she does not avoid or skirt what needs to be done.

## Ability to Complete

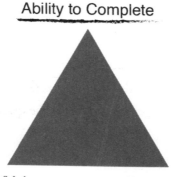

Ability to Complete

Attitude/Values                    Performance

Walter is a great employee. He is aligned with the company's core values. He performs his job well. But the projects he works on never seem to get finished on time, if at all. He sets time-specific objectives with Susan, his manacoach, and when Susan checks in on a weekly basis, Walter says that his projects are on track. But when the deadline comes, Walter can never bring any of his projects to completion.

It's all well and good if a team member has the right attitude, shares the same cultural values, and gets, wants, and can do the job. But what if that team member can't bring anything to completion? What if every time this team member sets a goal or an objective, you (as the manacoach) know that you can't rely on it, because you've never seen this person complete a commitment?

A great question might be, "If a person can't bring things to completion, isn't that an issue of capacity?" Let's talk about capacity versus commitment. Bill and Jane are bookkeepers. In their respective companies, both agree to implement a new software system within ninety days. Both are the right people in terms of core values and attitude, and both have the capacity to be great bookkeepers. They both "get" their job, both "want" their job, and both have "capacity," in terms of knowing the ins and outs of bookkeeping like the back of their respective hands. The difference is that because she is so good at managing her commitments, when Jane says she will complete something by a certain time, everyone knows that unless there is a catastrophe, Jane will complete it sooner than she says. This is not the case with Bill, who is not quite as good in managing his commitments. When he says a project will be finished by a certain time, it's a coin toss. It's not that Bill can't better manage his commitments; he just doesn't do it.

You must have a conversation regarding *critical expectations*. As a team manacoach, you must hold people accountable for bringing assigned tasks to completion, and if they aren't doing so, you need to address it. The formula is the same. The manacoach writes a letter stating the expectation and listing three or more specific examples where tasks have not been brought to completion on time. The manacoach sits down with the team member, has the critical conversation, and then delivers the letter.

## Firing: The Very Last Resort

A concern about your team member will always fall into one or more of the three areas of the triangle, and by following this model, you will never have difficulty identifying where to begin a dialogue of discovery to figure out where the problem lies. We have regular performance reviews because we all want to know where we stand in any relationship.

Remember that if employees know they aren't meeting expectations, they will almost always figure out a way to meet the standards or else leave your team (or the organization itself).

On the extremely rare occasion when you have to let someone go, follow these six steps:

1. At the beginning of the employee's workweek, bring her into a room with one other person, usually someone from HR or someone who you report to. It's widely accepted that you should allow people the opportunity to plunge right into action in response to the news that they no longer have a job, which is why we do this at the start of the workweek. Letting them go at the end of the week means they are stuck facing a weekend where they can't seek advice from professionals like career counselors, banks and other services are closed, and they can't make calls to other potential employers.

2. Inform the employee that her services are no longer needed. There is no need to (and it's recommended not to) go into detail or an explanation of any kind. If you did your job properly up to this point, the employee should know why. If you start giving reasons or justifications, an argument will most likely occur, and emotions could run high. Stick to your script. "There is no need for your services any longer." You could be tempted to go further into explanations, but don't.

3.      Have a check prepared for work done to date, holiday pay, benefit reimbursement, and so on. If severance is being offered, you are not paying it at this point.

4.      Have a release written by your lawyer, and inform the employee that she should take the release and discuss it with someone outside the company. Inform her that once she has returned all property and a signed copy of the release, the company will provide the severance that is offered in the documentation. Do not allow the employee to sign the release at the meeting.

5.      It's always best to escort the employee off the premises. This protects the company and the employee.

6.      When you make an announcement to the staff, simply inform them that the company had to make a change and provide no details. If everyone knows what is expected of them, and you have a history where your team members always know where they stand, nobody on your team will be surprised or seek out more information.

     I remember, long ago, when someone on our team was let go. He wasn't a great performer, but he had been with the company for over sixteen years. I went to my manacoach and asked him for the details. None were provided, but my manacoach asked if I respected him, and if I trusted him. The answer to those two questions was *yes*. Then he asked me if I thought he would ever fire someone if it wasn't critical to the team moving forward. The answer was *no*. I walked away knowing that my manacoach was a professional and that he wouldn't share specifics about my performance if I was ever let go from the team.

Terminating a team member is stressful, but the good news is that you will rarely have to fire anyone if you have the courage to address issues as they occur and identify and document them as outlined in this chapter. From close to three decades of experience, in thousands of businesses in every industry you can think of, we can assure you that what is recommended in this chapter works.

# CHAPTER 8 FOLLOW-UP

Five things to remember:

1.  Evaluating and addressing soft skills (attitude and values) is the most difficult because it addresses the person, not the skill sets in doing the job.

2.  You must be clear with specific examples in addressing these types of issues.

3.  Addressing attitude/value issues is where we are most prone to procrastinate. Don't.

4.  Unless there is something inherently wrong with an employee, in the rare event where you have to fire him/her, if the employee is surprised and upset, you have failed as a manacoach.

5.  If you are a manacoach and you find that you enjoy addressing these types of issues or you enjoy terminating someone, you are in the wrong position.

# The Four Simple Steps to Avoid Firing

(This "simple" but not "easy" process is
a proven way to avoid firing.)

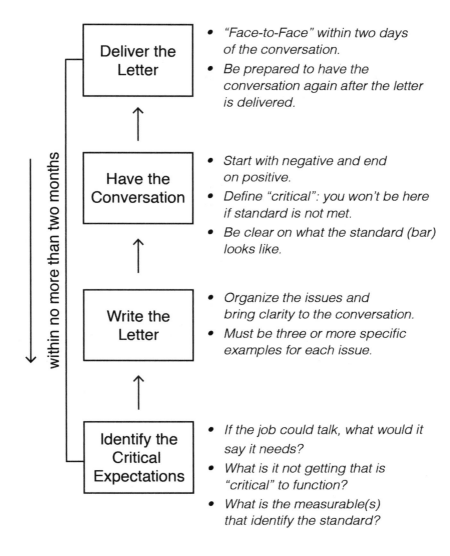

**Deliver the Letter**
- *"Face-to-Face" within two days of the conversation.*
- *Be prepared to have the conversation again after the letter is delivered.*

**Have the Conversation**
- *Start with negative and end on positive.*
- *Define "critical": you won't be here if standard is not met.*
- *Be clear on what the standard (bar) looks like.*

**Write the Letter**
- *Organize the issues and bring clarity to the conversation.*
- *Must be three or more specific examples for each issue.*

**Identify the Critical Expectations**
- *If the job could talk, what would it say it needs?*
- *What is it not getting that is "critical" to function?*
- *What is the measurable(s) that identify the standard?*

*within no more than two months*

## *chapter 9*

# DELEGATING AND DEPENDENCE

*"No person will make a great business who wants to do it all himself or get all the credit."*

## —ANDREW CARNEGIE

Jack charges his clients $500 an hour, and he pays his assistant Jill $30 an hour. Jack makes his own travel arrangements, even though Jill has an impressive history of doing this for other executives, as highlighted in her resume. Jack complains that he can't grow his practice because he is too busy. Jill rolls her eyes when she sees Jack making his own travel arrangements, because she knows she could do it just as well or better, but she feels that if Jack wanted her to do it, he'd delegate it to her. Jack would have all sorts of time if he knew how to identify tasks that his assistant could easily do. Whether or not Jack is good at booking his own travel doesn't matter. He is the wrong person for that job. The hospital doesn't have a doctor take out the garbage.

Delegating is by far the biggest challenge for every manacoach. Depending on what study you review, 60 to 85 percent of employees feel that their boss could be off-loading duties to them. There is no question that almost every manacoach is doing some task that could be delegated to someone else.

Most of us have a need to improve; we must be constantly in a state of growth. But we can't focus on improvement unless we let go of the other things that use up all of our time. If we don't delegate properly, we will never know whether we have the right people. We won't know if they are learning what we are teaching, how to intrinsically motivate them, and if we are making the right decision in the rare event we have to fire someone. Although the manacoach is a person, and delegating is a process, they have the same goal: "getting things done *efficiently* and *effectively* through others." To accomplish this, there are some fundamentals we need to review.

## Dependence: You Get What You Put Up With!

People do not, will not, and cannot become independent on their own. In order for people to become independent, the person they are dependent on must first reject that dependence. To be a manacoach, you really need to understand and believe this.

There is only one thing we were born naturally motivated and able to do on our own: the ability to suck. I know that it sounds funny, and it often gets a good laugh in my talks. But that's all we are motivated to do when we are born, and it's why babies are in trouble if they don't get milk when they suck, because then they stop sucking.

What is the takeaway from this? If our mother did not reject our dependence on her breast for food, we would have continued to breast-feed until we were embarrassed to bring our friends home from college. Manacoaches must make this principle their mantra: *in order for your team members to become independent, you must first reject their dependence.*

Many great businesspeople, like Bill Gates, have pointed out that you learn nothing when you are talking. You can only learn when you are listening (or using another one of your senses to take in information). From that statement logically follows the idea that you can't be learning anything when you are answering questions. You can only be learning when you are *asking* questions, and the better the questions, the more you learn. In their book *Multipliers*, Liz Wiseman and Greg McKeown provide everything you need to know about asking good questions. Let's say I approach you, as my manacoach, seeking an answer. Although I'm dependent on you for the answer, I am controlling you as long as you answer my question.

The person who asks the question is the person in control. I most likely am not asking you a question to knowingly be in control. I might be asking you a question because I'm too lazy to seek the answer myself. Maybe I don't know how to find an answer, or I don't have the aptitude to figure out the answer, or I want to test you. But the point is that *when I'm asking you a question, I am controlling you.*

Children understand this concept, although perhaps not at a conscious level. They ask, "Why is the sky blue, Daddy?" not because they want to know why the sky is blue but because they now have your undivided attention—they are controlling you. And if you don't believe this, then ask yourself why more questions always follow after you answer the first one. To put this to the test, the next time a child asks you a question that has nothing to do with the current situation, ask her why she thinks the sky is blue. When she answers with "I don't know," point her in the direction of the resources where she can bring the answer back to you. Here, at a very simple level, you have just taken control and rejected dependence.

## Either You Are Managing Them or They Are Managing You

Have you ever had a manager that you controlled? You had a task to finish that you didn't like, for example, so you approached your manager posing a difficult problem in the form of a question, and as a result your manager took the task off your hands. Later, while your manager was back at the office working on your undesirable task, you and the other workers laughed about it at the bar. Your manager didn't know it, but you were delegating something to him. I learned early on from Jim Renahan that there are three reasons why some managers do not delegate:

1. **They are insecure.** They don't want others to know too much about their job, because then what would they do? The reasoning here goes, "If you become better at what I do, then I will be let go, because they won't need me anymore." They might think that others aren't capable, and they are too insecure to explore that assumption further. They might like the feeling of having so many others depending on them. They might think they are irreplaceable and not want others to join them in that ranking. They might be control freaks and simply unable to let go. Regardless of how their insecurities manifest, insecure people will not delegate, and as long as that insecurity prevails, they will never be a manacoach. Remember in chapter 6 on vulnerability: those who are willing to be vulnerable are wholehearted. How can one be wholehearted and insecure at the same time?

2. **They don't know how**. Delegating is easy when you trust that the other person can do the task. But when you aren't sure or know they can't, you must either be able to teach it yourself or have a resource to teach it for you. To teach it yourself, you have to be able to break it down into components, delegate it a bit at a time, and then let go of it. The lack of ability to teach (or find others to teach) and to let go of tasks holds many of us back from being manacoaches.

3. **They don't want to go home**. Some people just like working or prefer being at work, perhaps due to a bad or no home life. Although companies like employees who want to work long hours, it is not healthy for those people, and therefore it is not healthy for the team or for the company. And remember that if you are working long hours and your team is not, by the very definition, you are not a manacoach.

## Insecurities with Delegating

I remember, in my early years, passing a graveyard with my grandfather. He would point at it and say, "A lot of the people under those tombstones thought they were irreplaceable in this world." For me, that story relates to the disappointing manager who doesn't want to delegate for fear of losing what he considers his stronghold or advantage in some area of expertise that nobody else has. The fear might stem from being replaced, or just the great feeling of being in control, but here is the problem: unless you are a skilled therapist, it's very difficult to identify where this insecurity stems from, and therefore it is very difficult to fix. Regardless, we know that people cannot be manacoaches if they are insecure.

We are all insecure to varying degrees. It feels good to be valued for what we know; it feels even better to be wanted and appreciated. And holding the winning hand when nobody else can see all the cards is one of the best feelings in the world. The problem is that a manacoach is not supposed to be playing the game. She's supposed to be managing the players in the best way possible—putting the right people in the right seats—because she knows that the team is only as strong as its weakest member.

If what holds you back from delegating is concern over what will be left for you to do, I encourage you to think of all the things you must achieve this month. If you could immediately delegate everything that comes to mind today, what would you work on tomorrow? The reality is that you would be doing much more insightful and productive work that is more of a challenge for you and more beneficial for your organization.

Dan Sullivan is the coach's coach in North America. He is a guru for many business coaches. He encourages everyone to discover his or her "unique ability." Better yet, retain a good coach to help you identify your unique abilities. Imagine a life where every day you get to do what you do best, which usually are those things you love to do. I say "usually" with this caveat: just because you love to do something doesn't necessarily mean that you are great at it. *American Idol* and other televised talent shows have demonstrated that just because you love to do something doesn't necessarily mean that you are good at it.

But if you love to do something, and your peers agree that you are in fact great at it, then the better you get at delegating, the more you get to spend time growing people and the organization with your unique abilities.

## Not Knowing How to Delegate

As seen in our conclusive research, just because you are great or a leader at something doesn't mean you can teach it. I was a terrible trumpet player, yet I produced award-winning high school wind ensembles. I had some great mentors in life who taught me to use exceptional students to demonstrate what I was teaching and to find outside help if I wasn't getting results. My experience has taught me that great people are always willing to help, but you have to ask. When asked for the secret behind his success, Chip Wilson, the man behind Lululemon, responded by saying he was never afraid to ask for help.

As a manacoach, if you are trying to teach a skill set to someone, you don't need to demonstrate it. In fact, even if you can demonstrate it but know someone who can do it better, you are doing your trainee a disservice by demonstrating it, because you are setting the ceiling on how well the skill can be carried out.

To delegate something, you must have the ability and resources to teach it. Manacoaches have the ability to teach by taking a step back, looking at all the things that are going wrong, and picking out the one thing that will make everything better if improved.

I have a great golf coach: Juan Rostworowski. His philosophy is clear: keep things simple. In the seven years that I've worked with Juan, he has only demonstrated something twice for me, and that was because I didn't believe what he was telling me was true so I asked him to show me. Through studying management and coaching, I've learned that great teachers only get you to focus on one or at most two concepts when they are teaching a skill. For example, Juan will look at my swing, and even though there might be four or five things going wrong, he gets me to focus on only one. When I focus on that one thing, everything else gets better. He might say, "Loosen your hands . . . pretend you have a baby bird in your hands instead of the club." "Are your hands as loose at the end of the swing as they were at the beginning?" "Did you just crush the bird through the swing?" He focuses on this because it's impossible to swing hard and fast in golf if your hands are loose. What I've learned in studying coaching is if someone is teaching you something and you feel confused or frustrated at the end of the lesson, you need a new teacher.

One way to tell if you need to find a new teacher is if she is giving you too many things to think about and confusing you. I laugh when I hear a golf coach saying to her student, "Keep your back straight, don't bend your left arm, loosen your hands, start with your downswing with your hips rotating." By the time the student is swinging the club back, his nerves are frazzled. If all your coach can do is demonstrate, she doesn't understand the concept of what she is teaching. In other words, she can do it herself, but she doesn't understand how to teach it.

The ability to teach skill sets is a talent, and nobody defines talent better than Marcus Buckingham does in *First Break All the Rules*. He conducted a twenty-year analysis of data collected from the Gallup organization. He found that we should not be forcing people to work on things that they don't have a talent for (they don't "get it"). We talked about this concept in the chapter on hiring (chapter 7), where people can be divided into two groups: "paper-oriented or process-oriented" people and "people" people. Those two groups would then be subdivided into introverts and extroverts.

With the odd exception, an introverted, paper-oriented person likes to analyze. She has a motto—"facts are facts"—and all the talk in the world doesn't matter to her if the data does not support the conclusion. She loves digging into processes and making certain that everything balances or adds up. Going into large groups of people she doesn't know creates stress. She likes to follow rules and principles. She has a talent for step-by-step thinking, and she must be given time to organize her thoughts. Her pessimism is a positive attribute in checking facts and figures because the numbers speak for themselves.

The extroverted people person is the opposite. He's optimistic and he'd much rather talk about a concept than look at numbers. He looks forward to meeting new people—the more, the better. It stresses him to keep track of numbers and documents.

If this is all you knew about each person, who do you think would have more talent for the sales seat, and who would have the talent for the accounting seat? Buckingham distinguishes between "management" and "leadership." His concepts are groundbreaking because he proves that we must stop making people work on their weaknesses. Dan Sullivan calls it a "unique ability" and Buckingham calls it "talent," but it doesn't matter what the term is. The manacoach is good at recognizing talent, and she delegates to those who possess the required talent. The person assigned the task can develop and feel a genuine sense of contributing, and as a result the team and organization grow as well.

The manacoach knows that people can learn only one thing, or at most two things, at a time. The next time your manager is trying to teach you something and you feel nothing but confusion, ask yourself this: is too much being thrown at you at once? Or if your coach is insisting that you work on something that you are weak at (setting you up for failure), our advice is to tell the coach what you are feeling. If the teaching doesn't show any improvement, which usually is the case, run as fast as you can and find a new manager or company to work for.

## Not Wanting to Go Home

You won't find a true manacoach working alone in his office late at night unless his team members are working as well. In every business cycle, for every function, there are busy times where there's more work than can be done in normal working hours. But if a manacoach gets things done efficiently and effectively through others, why would he ever work long hours alone? If the only conclusion is that he doesn't have a life outside work, then he will eventually burn out, not to mention reaching his ceiling in the organization.

Unfortunately, nothing can be done when the reason for someone taking on work that should be delegated is that she doesn't want to go home. This is a personal matter, but the organization should let the individual know that working long hours alone, without her team, is not impressing anyone. It is not helping the company grow and achieve its goals. The manager needs to have a life outside the business to maintain a healthy lifestyle.

## Rejecting the Dependence

Jack is a manacoach, and his team members know never to ask a question unless they have a proposed solution. If they ask Jack a question, he will respond every time with, "What would you do if I wasn't here?" Jack has made it clear that no team member is paid to have "Jack think for you." If your proposed solution doesn't make sense to Jack, he will ask you questions so you can address the problems with your solution. Jack will then help you solve your problem, or if time permits, he might send you off to find another solution that makes better sense. Once you understand Jack's position—to help you only with your solution—you learn to devise a proposed solution before approaching Jack. You always feel safe discussing issues with him, and although at times you feel your solutions are weak, Jack may very well tell you that your proposed solution is better than anything he can come up with.

With this simple strategy, Jack knows how his team members perform in different situations. Because he knows this, he realizes which tasks can be delegated and which cannot. If you develop a habit of answering every question with, "What would you do if I wasn't here?" then you will be well on your way to being a top manacoach, and your life will improve measurably. You will learn things about your teammates you never knew.

## Follow Up

Dave reports to Jill, a weak manager. She is always asking Dave to do some new task or to work on a project unrelated to his day-to-day duties, but nine times out of ten, Jill never mentions those projects again. After a while, Dave learned not to work on something Jill assigned until she followed up, because Jill would probably forget about it. He learned that she is disorganized and/or absentminded.

You don't want to be known by your team as the "flavor of the day" manager. You lose all credibility with your team if you don't follow up. The manacoach must be organized, or she will lose the respect of her team members. You don't want to be frustrated, because none of your team members take you seriously. No follow-ups, no results.

Our research has pinpointed five of the most common reasons managers give for not delegating. All five also fall under Jim Renahan's three reasons why a person does not delegate. Here are those five reasons:

1.   **Trust (insecurity)**—If you are not delegating because you don't trust your team members, then the question you must

focus on is *why*. Is it because you have been let down by others in the past or because the team members have given you reason not to trust them? If you are unable to trust, then you have to "work on you," and being a manacoach is out of the question until this is resolved. As discussed in the chapter on vulnerability (chapter 6), you might not even know why you don't trust others—the answer might be buried so far inside you that you can't identify it. A team cannot move forward together without trust. Every manacoach knows this and knows that the process starts with them. If a manacoach doesn't trust others, then he won't be trusted. As my good friend Don Tinney of EOS Worldwide says, "Trust is not a condition, it's a decision." You decide if you are willing to trust someone.

On the other hand, if you don't trust an underperforming team member who has let you down in the past, this means you haven't followed the steps about critical conversations laid out in chapter 8. Trust is the foundation of communication, and communication cannot operate without trust. Remember too that trust is impossible unless a manacoach demonstrates a constant level of integrity. So a related question is, do you walk your talk?

2.  **Fear (insecurity)**—Delegating is a risky business. There is always a risk that the person you are delegating to will screw up. Tom Peters always said that great managers (manacoaches) only need to do two things well: Shut up, and let go. Letting go requires a huge leap of faith. Every book you read on delegating will have the phrase "let go" in it. Just remember: *you wouldn't hold the position you have now if someone in your past didn't take a leap of faith with you.*

Already you have pictures of mentors that are flashing in your mind. They put their fears and uncertainties to the side and took a chance on you, and now it's time for you to take a deep breath, let go, and pay it forward to another talented person wanting to develop. The manacoach grows people, and people can't grow with a noose (your fears) around their necks.

3.  **Cost (inability to teach)**—Delegating can be a costly business if the person being assigned the responsibility fails. At first glance, it seems that every time you delegate to someone, it's going to cost the organization more than doing it yourself. The best-kept secret in business is that growth costs money. If a lawyer is worth $400 an hour to the firm and his assistant is worth $50 an hour, the lawyer costs the firm money every time she does a task that her assistant could be doing. Granted, the assistant takes time to get up to speed, and this imposes a cost. But once the assistant has mastered the assignment, return on investment is at least eight-fold.

    My favorite question to business owners is, "What is your time worth?" As a manacoach, you might think your time is only worth what you are getting paid. But the real question is, "What is your time worth to the organization?" If you are worth hundreds of dollars per hour to the organization, and someone on your team who is paid far less than you could do the task, what are you costing the organization by not delegating?

    It's difficult to determine the long-term cost to an organization when a manacoach does not delegate. But we know that an organization's growth cannot be sustained if its people aren't growing, and people aren't growing if skill sets and roles aren't being transferred.

4. **Incompetence or inability (don't know how to teach)** —Incompetence or inability takes us back to the chapter on hiring (chapter 7). If an employee truly lacks the ability to do what you are delegating, why is he working for you? Have you really tested his abilities, or is the issue that you are not letting go? The manacoach has a response to every question asked by team members: What would you do if I weren't here? The manacoach creates a culture of thinking by always asking this question. The manacoach must first reject the dependence of her team members in order for them to achieve independence. You cannot determine competence or ability without first rejecting dependence.

5. **No time (insecurity or don't know how to teach)** —"It's faster if I do it myself." Have you ever heard your inner voice saying that to you? This is what we call the "pain process" in delegating. Think of watching a child tie his shoelaces; you could save so much time by jumping in and doing it yourself. Instead, as Tom Peters says, you "shut up" and bite your lip until it bleeds. If you bide your time, it won't be long until the person is tying his own shoelaces. In the meantime, think of the rewards of that pain and frustration. Now you have more time to do what you do best because of the time you save from not having to tie everyone's shoelace. Sure, there are times of risk or time constraints where you have to step in. Your child is tying his shoelaces agonizingly slow, and perhaps you are running late. Tie the shoe yourself, but never forget that no growth occurred in that instance. You

will be tying those shoelaces for the rest of your life or until you finally shut up and let go.

Remember that another primary objective as a manacoach is to grow people, and when you answer a question or do something for someone, nobody is growing. If you don't take the time to delegate, you won't have the time for your own growth as a manacoach. That is a fact.

# CHAPTER 9 FOLLOW-UP

1.  Do my team members know not to come to me with a problem unless they have a proposed solution?

2.  Am I constantly evaluating what my team members love to do and what they are great at so that we are all working with our strengths in getting the job done?

3.  Do I realize that my role as a manacoach is to grow people? If I'm answering questions instead of asking them, nobody is growing, and I am the barrier.

*c h a p t e r  1 0*

# COMMUNICATION

*"Electric communication will never be a substitute for the face of someone who with their soul encourages another person to be brave and true."*

## —CHARLES DICKENS

How did people communicate in the time of Dickens? We have since reached greater heights in communication than anyone from that era could have ever predicted. Now there are many different types of electrical devices with incredible computing power that allow us to explore all aspects of communication. At the push of a button, we can instantly send videos as well as verbal and written messages to millions of people around the planet. The devices available to us today were only props on science fiction movies not so long ago.

But here is a question involving these advances that I love to ask audiences: With all of the advances in our technology, have we become better or worse at communicating with each other?

If you think we've become worse, you are far from being alone. You might have a million friends on the Internet, but how many friends do you really have? When the chips are down, how many would watch your back?

Getting the best out of people means removing their obstacles and understanding them, their challenges, and their issues. Team success depends on a group of people working together, each accountable for their well-defined function on the team. Manacoaches know that it's extremely inefficient and time-wasting to diagnose and solve issues through the written word. The manacoach and her teammates must talk to each other—they don't write each other.

## Quit Hiding behind Your Keyboard!

The problem with the written word is that we can't interpret the tone. In illustrating this in our seminars, we like to write these two words on a board: "nice dress." The question we pose is, if I communicate these two words to a woman in the room wearing a dress, is it a positive, complimentary message, or is it a negative, critical message? The answer is that it depends on the tone. Picture me saying "nice dress" in a cynical tone, talking out the side of my mouth and rolling my eyes. The tone completely changes the message.

There is no reliable research data to identify exactly how much of corporate communication between employees is in writing versus face-to-face or on the phone. It's becoming all too common to hear stories that involve an argument or an issue with another employee that is conducted entirely through e-mail correspondence. We can only shake our heads in disbelief that two employees within fifty feet of each other can't have a face-to-face conversation. I used to think that it is extremely difficult to solve issues without a face-to-face conversation, and now I believe that it's impossible. Conversations over the phone help us to determine tone, but face-to-face is the best way to effectively communicate with someone.

For this reason, we try to instill the following mantra in every organization that we work with: if you are communicating a message of critique, negativity, or disagreement, you must force yourself to do it face-to-face. If that isn't possible, then use a device where you can have a conversation—it used to be called a telephone. Today's cell phones and websites allow you to have a remote video conversation that is nearly as direct.

A manacoach should resist the temptation to take the easy way out and communicate his concerns, disapproval, or critique through the written word. It doesn't work. In fact, it's dangerous. Communicating with the written word is a great tool if we are simply conveying information (e.g., confirmations for meetings, answers to quick questions, times to choose from for the next event, etc.).

Would Herb Brooks be considered one of the top coaches of all time if he cut Ralph Cox from the team through a letter, e-mail, or text? Words that come to mind are "pathetic," "weak," and "cowardly," to list a few.

Another thing I find interesting is the assumption that everyone receives digital messages immediately after they are sent. The other day I was accused of not being prepared for a significant meeting. The relevant materials were not sent to me until late Friday afternoon to review for the meeting, which was at 8 a.m. on the following Monday. The meeting materials were sent to my assistant, who had already gone home early on Friday afternoon. She never saw the documents in time to forward me the e-mail containing what I needed to review. I never received the meeting materials or even knew that they existed until I was scolded for being unprepared. Even if the meeting materials had been sent out in a timely manner and my assistant was able to forward me the e-mail, who is to say it didn't go directly to junk mail without my knowledge?

It can be a similar situation with a cell phone. Sometimes I'll receive a batch of text messages all at once—that were sent over a three-day period. I respond to each message as fast as I can, but people still get mad because I didn't respond sooner. Yet the reason I didn't respond in a timely fashion was because the messages weren't received until a day or two after they were sent.

Are we becoming so consumed with our electronic gadgets that we are hiding behind all of our technological advancements? Could we, in a sense, be spoiled by how powerful these advancements have made us? Charles Dickens understood the dangers of electric communication over 150 years ago . . . why can't we?

## Dare to Enter the Danger

For over two decades I have counseled presidents and business owners, and most of the time I spend with them is helping them prepare for tough conversations. Tough conversations are those that deal with delivering criticism or negative news. Being a manacoach is not for the weak or faint of heart. The uncertainty involved in having tough conversations with people is stressful.

It takes courage, and I mean real courage, to have tough conversations. If you have ever meant to criticize someone and then avoided it, you are not alone. I remember many situations when I intended to have a tough conversation with someone, yet as I was walking to his office, I turned around and walked the other way. The most difficult part of a tough conversation is starting it.

Manacoaches have not only this courage but also have deep, caring empathy for their teammates. Think back to great coaches you spent time with in the past. Did you trust them to come and tell you when something was wrong, or were you stung by that e-mail or memo where they cited something you did wrong? Did they watch your back and not talk to anyone behind your back, or did they send you notes putting you down while copying everyone in the office on the e-mail? Did they understand you?

The strategy we use on how to enter the danger zone comes from Joseph Grenny's bestselling *Crucial Conversations*. I have used Grenny's strategy, and I know it works. You start by communicating what you observe, making sure not to express any opinions or judgments. The next step is to articulate how what you've seen makes you feel. The last step is to clearly communicate what you need from that person to resolve the issue. I strongly recommend that you read Grenny's book, because there are a lot of places in these steps where you can get into trouble. Although it sounds simple, like anything effective, this process is definitely not easy when it comes to crucial conversations.

I write a letter before the conversation, and I strongly encourage all of my clients to do the same. That way the issue is clear in my mind. I have a better idea what I need to say, and I can stay with a strategy of delivering the message. Writing a letter, as mentioned in the chapter on firing, is also useful because after the issues have been addressed, you can give the letter to the person. It's important for a manacoach to do this because a lot can be lost in a stressful conversation, and the manacoach knows that much can be misinterpreted.

Herb Brooks letting Ralph Cox go gives us an example of this three-part process. Based on Cox's recollection of the meeting, Brooks started by outlining what he observed. Cox was recovering from a five-month-old injury, and with the larger rink size in Europe, Brooks was concerned with Cox's ability to keep up. Brooks told Cox that it made him feel terrible. He was sad, stressed, and it was one of the toughest decisions he had to make in his life. Finally, Brooks needed Cox to understand that if he were allowed twenty-one players, it wouldn't be an issue. He needed Cox to vacate his position on the team, but he needed him to understand that it had nothing to do with who Cox was as a person.

This is how a manacoach treats people. It's decent, respectful, and simple, but it's never easy. If you can't have these types of conversations—if they're too hard, or if you don't think you have what it takes—then here is my plea one more time: please, don't manage people!

If people aren't communicating, it's because they don't trust you. This might not be your fault. You may have inherited a position where your predecessor didn't walk his talk. You may have inherited a situation where people never knew where they stood and nobody addressed the hard issues—everything was swept under the carpet. You might have inherited a culture where people talk about other people all the time. Trust is interesting in that you can spend years building it with someone, but a single event can destroy it. People have to trust that you have the strength to address issues face-to-face, both openly and honestly, before they feel safe to open up to you. They have to know that their secret is safe with you. This can take varying amounts of time.

The solution is simple (but never easy). Some people have a wish to end world hunger. Along with solving world hunger, my wish is that every organization worldwide would address the tough issues face-to-face, eyeball-to-eyeball. I wish that every person in every organization would be conscious that they are breaking the golden rule when they are justifying, criticizing, judging, or being negative through the written word.

## Interpretation

Say this out loud to a group of people the next time you are at a gathering: "Thirty cows in a field, twenty-eight chickens. How many didn't?" Then tell them the answer is ten. Then say it louder and ask them why they look so confused. Usually when people don't understand us, we are being misinterpreted. So we speak louder, to the point of yelling, because we erroneously think that the louder we talk, the better the chance we will be understood. The problem here is that they are misinterpreting what is being said. If they saw it written as "thirty cows in a field, twenty ate chickens," they would understand your answer.

The manacoach understands that people can misinterpret what's being said in a face-to-face conversation, and they can react accordingly. When you are trying to get something across to someone, and the person is quick to respond in a charged or aggressive manner, stop the conversation and ask that person what she heard. Look her straight in the eye and ask, "What did you hear me just say?"

More times than you can imagine, the response will be "twenty-eight chickens" instead of "twenty ate chickens." Too often, we allow ourselves to go down a rabbit hole in a conversation to the point that we aren't even talking about the same thing. Misinterpreting what's being said, we continue on in our dialogue based on different assumptions about the discussion. If ever in doubt, stop the conversation and confirm the assumptions by simply asking, "What did you hear me say?" This is always an automatic issue resolver.

Communication can only be useful if the message is clearly interpreted and understood by the receiver. How language is interpreted by our brains heavily depends on the culture people inhabit as they grow up. In different cultures, words and phrases can have completely different meanings. The manacoach needs to always be aware of this.

## Politics versus Accountability

Politics is the practice and the theory of influencing others. Here is the best way to understand the difference between being political and not being political. When you are being authentic, you are saying or doing something because that is what you believe to be right. You are not being political. When you are shaping your words or actions to influence a response, you are being political.

True leaders don't concern themselves with politics. They don't care about influencing others, whether they stand in front, at the side, or behind them. They look to the future and do what is required: the right thing.

Manacoaches, on the other hand, have to concern themselves with politics. They don't practice them; they manage them. Manacoaches know that when there is more than one person in the room, things can go political, where one is trying to influence the other. But manacoaches also know a very important principle. Politics and accountability cannot live in the same space together. Politics is inversely related to accountability—the more accountability, the less the politics, and vice versa. Yet despite the fact that this is an extremely simple fact, managing according to this principle can be very difficult.

# The Inverse Relationship Between Accountability and Politics

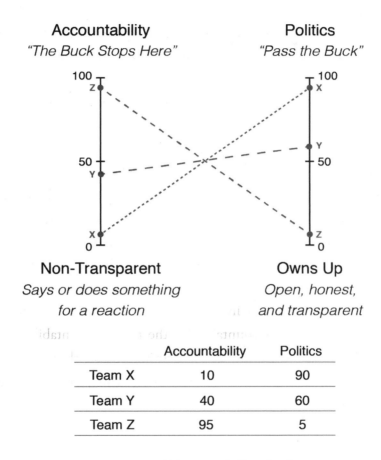

| | Accountability | Politics |
|---|---|---|
| Team X | 10 | 90 |
| Team Y | 40 | 60 |
| Team Z | 95 | 5 |

**Accountability and politics can't live in the same room.**

Politics existing in an environment of accountability is like a human living in an environment without oxygen—it isn't possible. Think about an environment you have experienced where people are more worried about what people are saying than they are about what the job requires. Did the people in that culture know what their key accountabilities were? Did they know how they were being measured? Did they have specific tasks that had to be completed by a hard deadline? The manacoach knows that if he does not communicate these accountabilities, he is inviting politics to enter the workplace. People start to fight for position by influencing others rather than by getting the job done.

Let's take the situation of a kid on a basketball team who doesn't understand the function of her position. Say she is assigned the position of guard, and nobody explains the key functions of this position. There are two questions we need to ask ourselves. The first is, if she doesn't know what her key functions are, how can she be held accountable? And the second question addresses the dangers for the team: what will she do to make herself useful in her own mind while she is not being held accountable? You leave her with no choice but to create situations that are political. In business, if your salesperson doesn't know what his key functions are on the team and what you are holding him accountable for (or he does know, but you aren't holding him to account), what are you leaving him free to do?

People need to know where they stand—that's it. One of the single most important roles for the manacoach is having good communications skills and courage in fulfilling that need. The effective manacoach upholds a culture where people have to discuss issues face-to-face rather than e-mailing or texting them and where people are clear on their accountabilities, the expected standards regarding accountability, and the consequences for not meeting those standards. The manacoach promotes a culture that communicates, works hard and together as a team, and where people don't have to revert to politics to influence and get recognized.

Sounds simple—it's not, if you want to be a true manacoach! It is an ongoing, lifelong struggle that is part of the job.

# CHAPTER 10 FOLLOW-UP

1.   Do you find that in your culture there are a lot of emails of a negative nature containing criticism and complaints where others are copied? If yes, what are you doing about it?

2.   Do you have what it takes or the desire and talent to have the tough conversations with the people you work with? If not, should you be a manacoach?

3.   Is your culture political? Does everyone know what they are accountable for and do they take full accountability when things go wrong? Keep those questions in your mind as you evaluate your culture and you will find that you can't answer "yes" to both.

*chapter 11*

# REWARDS AND PUNISHMENTS

*"...I did not let the fear of death govern my life; and my reward was, I had my life. You are going to let the fear of poverty govern your life; and your reward will be that you will eat, but you will not live."*

**—GEORGE BERNARD SHAW**

Often, when we are managing a group of people, we make the mistake of punishing good behavior and rewarding bad behavior. Manacoaches have to watch for this on a constant basis.

Don't you just love it when you go into a mall and find out that the cell phone company you have done business with for years is offering a huge promotional gift that you cannot receive, because you already have an existing plan? I like to approach the rep, advise him that I've been a loyal customer for eleven years, and ask for the gift. The answer is always "No, it's only for new customers." So in the end, they are rewarding some person off the street and punishing me for my loyal business.

Here are some of the things manacoaches stay focused on to avoid rewarding bad behavior:

1.  Although tempting, don't lecture a group of people on a rule or procedure that is not being followed when only one or a few in the group are the culprits. It's unproductive and demotivating, and it shows a lack of courage on your part. Pull the individuals that you are concerned about aside and address them. This might sound ridiculously obvious, but managers make this mistake all the time.

    I have been doing yoga for years, and one of the critical expectations is that no matter what, you stay in the room from beginning to end. The other day, a few students left the room for a few minutes, and while they were gone, the teacher went over the reasons why it was so important to stay in the room. She lectured us for a full five minutes. When the four students returned, we continued with the program. But they didn't have to listen to the lecture. They were rewarded, and we, the good ones who followed the rule, were punished.

2.  Don't offer rewards or incentives to stop unproductive or bad behavior. Look for ways to recognize and reward good behavior. You want your team focused on the latter.

    For example, let's assume team members who smoke are less productive. They take more breaks, and they take more sick days. How can you address this issue as a manacoach? What is the right approach for a manacoach to end this undesirable habit? A method that has worked in the past is offering the employees who smoke an incentive, usually money, if they successfully stop smoking for a year. As a manacoach in this situation, though, you have to ask yourself, "Why are you rewarding undesired behavior and punishing desired behavior?" You have to look at the bigger picture and realize that the team members who smoke are getting a reward by ceasing to do an undesired behavior, and the rest of your more productive employees get nothing.

3.      If you don't see a change in the bad behavior, deal with it on an individual basis, and if it doesn't change, take further steps immediately. Once a team sees that unproductive behavior is acceptable, it spreads like wildfire.

With team building in mind, if the undesired behavior is rampant and your team thinks it's acceptable, the manacoach will react by punishing the team as a whole. If you ever do this, be sure that the culprits are in attendance and the whole team knows what they are being punished for while emphasizing who was responsible for all of this extra effort. Manacoaches do this in sports. When the team has an unproductive practice, the manacoach extends the practice with extra drills.

Herb Brooks is portrayed doing this in *Miracle*. During a pre-Olympic game in Sweden, Herb noticed a couple of players flirting with some girls in the stands while they were playing. After the game was over and everyone was leaving, Herb returned the team to the ice and made them run drills ("Herbies") until they almost collapsed from exhaustion. His point was that the team could not succeed unless everyone was focused on the game.

## Why Bonuses and Profit Sharing Don't Work in Most Cases

For over two decades and in over two hundred companies, we have witnessed the frustration of business owners and manacoaches who try to motivate team members with incentives and rewards. This frustration comes because of mixed results, such as when the owner thinks the employees are ungrateful, the performance decreases, and/or the team members end up being more discouraged than encouraged.

Any research worth its weight in gold touts the benefits of employee recognition. The data is out there, but we continue to ignore it. To allow your team members to think and contribute, you should clearly communicate what you want in terms of results (expectations), as opposed to how you think it should be done (process). You have to recognize that your team members are individuals who value different things. When you consider that we all value different things, it's no wonder that a one-size-fits-all monetary bonus scheme doesn't work.

You can avail yourself of assessment tools that can tell what an individual values. Some people have a utilitarian attitude and value "return on investment." Others value the environment around us, helping others, going to church, learning new things, or understanding how something works.

A few years ago, I attended board meetings where the owner of a business was frustrated. His software developer was not completing a desperately needed, major project. The board, comprised of business owners, engineers, and finance experts, suggested that the owner offer the software person a $5,000 bonus if he completed the project by the end of the month. When we met the next month, it still wasn't finished.

One board member suggested a values assessment, which is like a behavior assessment that identifies what a person values. The assessment told us that the developer in question had a high "aesthetic" value. When the business owner learned that the software developer valued the quality of his surroundings more than money, the owner offered a new reward of $1,500 to decorate the developer's office and buy whatever he needed to make his surroundings more comfortable. The project was finished faster than promised.

Now, if you value money above all else, this approach makes no sense to you. Why would a person be satisfied with something that costs $1,500 when he could have had $5,000? The point is that as humans, what we value doesn't have to make sense. Yet if the reward doesn't target what we value, we won't respond in a positive way toward it, and we certainly won't be motivated by it.

## The Carrot and Stick Method Doesn't Work

Daniel Pink has conducted research that explains the two decades of frustration we witnessed concerning the failure of bonuses and profit sharing. Daniel tells us that the carrot and stick approach to increasing production only works in certain situations. After reading his bestselling book *Drive*, you will have no doubt as to why.

What Pink has proven through a number of reliable findings is not groundbreaking: team members want to feel like their contributions are important. They want to be challenged to think. They want to be recognized when they have a good idea. They want to know where they stand and if they are meeting or exceeding agreed-upon expectations. These common-sense principles, though, are constantly ignored in many companies.

In the chapter on delegating, we discussed "rejecting dependence." Remember that when a team member asks a question, you should respond, "What would you do if I wasn't here?" If the team member gives you a solution that is even better than what you were thinking, what happens? Watch her heart and soul glimmer through her eyes when you respond with, "Wow! Jane, that was a much better solution than I was thinking. Thank you so much!" And as she walks away two feet off the ground, ask yourself if a bonus, a pair of theater tickets, or a gift certificate for a dinner could replace her feeling of self-worth that resulted from your kind words and recognition.

We know that employees will take a reduction in pay to work for the type of manacoach who challenges them to think and recognizes them when they go above and beyond. So as Daniel Pink constantly asks, why do we keep offering incentives and rewards that don't work? Why does business keep doing what science knows doesn't work? Of course, your team members have to be paid in line with the market, but your job as a manacoach is to grow people. And you can only grow them through well-communicated expectations and constant recognition when those expectations are met.

The carrot and stick approach can only work if we have a bunch of horses *mindlessly* running in the same direction.

# CHAPTER 11 FOLLOW-UP

1. In terms of rewarding someone, think back to a time when someone shook your hand, looked you in the eye, and congratulated you on doing something great. Now go back to how that felt and ask yourself, honestly, if money could recreate that feeling?

2. The next time someone asks you for a raise or you are allocating bonuses, ask yourself what you are paying for and if you are actually going to get it?

A gift ceases to be a gift when it is expected. When you give someone a gift because you like the way things are going, then call it a gift. If you are paying for increased performance, be sure all parties know exactly what that means, have direct control over outcomes, and agree on how it will be measured.

*c h a p t e r   1 2*

# BE BOLD AND BE S.M.A.R.T.

*"When it is obvious that the goals cannot be reached, don't adjust the goals, adjust the action steps."*

## —CONFUCIUS

Manacoaches remove barriers and grow people, because if people aren't growing, the team isn't growing, and if the team isn't growing, the organization is dying. And if that is the role of the manacoach, then common sense dictates that the manacoach must be a master at communicating and monitoring expectations.

Any expectation that is not achieved is a goal or objective to shoot for. A goal is thought to be long term, and an objective is achieved in the shorter term. Both are smaller steps in the big picture of what needs to be built.

## Be S.M.A.R.T.

All expectations must have conditions or assumptions that are defined as clearly as possible so that the goals are fully understood by the people helping to achieve them. To ensure a good result, expectations must be S.M.A.R.T.

Specific

Measurable

Attainable

Realistic

Time-bound

I have worked with hundreds of managers who knew the acronym but didn't practice it or really understand it. I promise that understanding and executing it properly will improve team performance.

**Specific:** What is the outcome? What has to be done? Think about this statement as an example of an objective: "We are going to start looking for a salesperson." I was working with a management team in a remote area, and there was a beautiful patio outside the meeting room. While they were discussing how to look for a salesperson, I got up, walked out on the deck, and looked around. I then came back in and announced to everyone that the objective had been accomplished. I had gone out on the deck and "looked" for a salesperson, so the objective was achieved. Although it seems silly, it was the manager's fault for not being more specific.

"I am going to hire a salesperson." "I am going to hire a search firm and have three people shortlisted for this position." "I am going to develop a job description for the position of sales rep and present it to the team." These are all specific objectives. It is clear to me what has to be satisfied in order for these objectives to be achieved.

**Measurable:** If it can't be measured, it can't be managed. How can we tell if the objective is achieved or not achieved? Is it qualitative or quantitative? If it's quantitative, then it's usually easy to measure. But if it's qualitative, don't move forward until everyone is satisfied on how success will be determined. It's that simple.

One of my clients wanted his receptionist to improve how she answered phones and greeted people. This seems like a difficult objective to measure, but he devised a way. Every quarter, his company would contact five repeat customers and ask them, on a scale of one to ten, if they felt they were greeted in a professional and courteous manner when they came in or called in (ten was excellent). The receptionist must score at least eight on average to accomplish the objective.

It's interesting to note that many companies make the process too complicated, when in most cases, one simple metric is all that is needed. There is a way to measure almost every objective or expectation, and in those cases where you can't measure it, do not assign it or accept it.

**Achievable** or **Attainable** and **Relevant** or **Realistic:** For the manacoach to be effective, her goals must be both attainable and realistic. My favorite question is: what is the difference between "attainable" and "realistic"? Could I run a marathon in under 3:45 at my age? *Yes*. It is attainable. Am I going to give up the time to train, hire a good coach, and buy the right equipment to achieve this feat? *No*. This goal is attainable but not realistic.

Wikipedia and other sources state that "A" stands for "achievable" and "R" stands for "relevant." This is easier to understand. It's easier to see that a goal can be achievable but not relevant (or relevant but not achievable) than for something to be realistic but not attainable.

**Time-bound:** Many goals we come across don't have deadlines; this is where you can get into trouble. Say you agree on a goal, but six months later, it's still not finished. You are frustrated because you thought it should be finished in three months, but the person who accepted the responsibility thought it would take a year. The goal must have a mutually agreed-upon, specific, defined time period attached to it.

## What Are the Conditions?

Let's say you are my manager, and you want me to commit to completing a project by a certain time. The goal is both achievable and relevant to both of us, and we've agreed when it must be completed. If I'm wise, I will think of all of the conditions that must be met for this goal to be achieved. In this example, you want me to begin construction on the pool by January 1, and it's October 1. I would need to think about factors that could delay the project. With holidays like Thanksgiving and Christmas, getting permits could be very difficult at that time of year. Additionally, one of my best workers has been diagnosed with an illness. He's fit to work for now, but he will have to take time off periodically. Realistically, both situations that have been identified could seriously delay the project and prevent me from meeting our goal.

Conditions always start with the word "given." Achieving the goal of starting the pool by January 1 is conditional on two factors, so for the sake of integrity, I would write the goal this way: given that permits are not unusually delayed due to government and statutory holidays and that Jack doesn't have to take more than a week of sick leave, we will have started the pool by January 1. This way if Jack is sick for a lot more time than we predicted or the permits are delayed for an excessive amount of time, I retain my reputation for being reliable, even though the goal wasn't met.

Here is what the manacoach is clear on: in any performance activity, such as business, every person on the team must know exactly what their role is and what goals they must achieve for the team to move forward.

# CHAPTER 12 FOLLOW-UP

1.  The objective must be so specific that a person off the street who knows nothing about your business can determine if the objective was achieved or not. "I'm going to 'look for' a salesperson" is accomplished if I stick my head out a window and gander. "I'm going to 'hire' a salesperson" leaves no question as to what has to be achieved.

2.  If it can't be measured, it can't be managed. Be sure that everything you assign can be measured in the end, even if it's "complete" or "not complete."

3.  If two people are responsible for an objective to be completed, nobody is. Whatever the objective, make sure that one person owns it and that one person agrees that it can be completed given the conditions. If you are the only one who thinks it's relevant and achievable, there needs to be further dialogue.

# concluding remarks

*"It can be frightening to think that we matter that much to other people. As long as we make leadership something bigger than us, as long as we keep leadership beyond us, as long as we make it about changing the world, we give ourselves an excuse not to expect it every day from ourselves and each other."*

## —DREW DUDLEY

I wrote this book from a dream that developed into a mission. We have allowed the term "leadership" to become an achievement for the chosen few, when in fact it's attainable by anyone who has the courage to look into the future and do the right thing, much like Rosa Parks did on December 1, 1955, when she refused to move from what was mandated by the government of the day to be a white person's seat on a public bus. Today it seems unbelievable that there was such a law, but there was at the time, she was breaking it, and she didn't care. Rosa Parks didn't manage anyone and didn't care who was beside her. She was prepared to break the law of the land. She was a true leader because she was doing what she thought was right.

I greatly appreciate the exchanges that Drew Dudley and I have had. In his talk on TED.com about leadership, he starts out with this thought-provoking question: "How many of you are completely comfortable with calling yourself a leader?" I like asking this question because few people in the audience raise their hands, just as few did in Drew's audience. This is because we've allowed ourselves to think that leadership is something much more than it is. Drew does a masterful nine-minute talk, bringing more clarity to this topic than I ever could. Watch his presentation, and you will understand what leadership is and is not. Interestingly enough, it's not about leading others, and it can be as simple as walking over and putting garbage into a can and securing it so the bears can't get at it.

Most of the best authors, professors, and entrepreneurs and CEOs in the business world use the words "leadership," "management," and "executives" interchangeably. They talk about leadership like it is something up above the clouds where only the chosen few can rise, and it drives me crazy.

## My Type of Leader

Unfortunately for our children, our definition of leadership is ambiguous at best, and a lot of examples they are exposed to are poor. Adolf Hitler was a raging narcissist and a monster. For years, Lance Armstrong misled his fans and bullied those who challenged him. For six months, Bill Clinton tried his best to cover up his blatant lies to the American public, not expecting that a woman would not have her blouse dry-cleaned. Unfortunately, the list continues and gets even more concerning. Their words might be inspiring, but their actions speak louder than their words. We have little use for politicians because we don't trust that their actions will align with their words. Many of us don't trust the food industry, pharmaceutical industry, or medical establishment because the people who supposedly lead these companies are more interested in return to shareholders than anything else.

The world is longing for people who are passionate about making humankind better and the world a better place to live. We long for people who look to the future without regard for the naysayers or those who only care about what's in it for them—we long for leaders who walk their talk. The courage they repeatedly demonstrate and the alignment of their actions with their words makes us feel safe and, therefore, we believe in them.

Leaders come in all varieties. They can be introverted or extroverted, have varying degrees of intelligence, be big or small, male or female, and eloquent and charismatic or quiet and unassuming. But let's be clear: the attributes that make them a great leader don't qualify them as a manacoach. Yet business continues to take the best performers and allow, force or persuade them to take a management position, even though the research is conclusive that there's a great chance that this simply won't work. What people do that makes them great may preclude them from getting things done efficiently and effectively through others.

Leaders don't have to understand people or be driven to learn what makes people tick, but make no mistake; these are critical skills for the manacoach.

The late John Wooden shows up on any list of top fifty coaches. He was humble yet strict. He cared more about his team than he cared about himself. His expectations were clear, and everyone on his teams always knew where they stood and how they were being measured. He was a leader and a manacoach. Wooden was a whole-hearted person who cared about people.

In sports and performance-based arts like theater, they never mix up the role of team coach and team leader. Few trumpet players sitting in the first seat of a great symphony orchestra dream of standing at the conductor's podium. Few great actors dream of being a director, and few great athletes dream of coaching a team, and if they do, they have less than a 20 percent chance of winning more games than they lose. The data doesn't lie.

## Final Thoughts on the Manacoach

As Mr. Wooden said, "conceit" should not be in the manacoach's vocabulary. Think of any great manacoach you have seen. The good ones are humble. You can't be committed to and good at growing people if you are focused on yourself. If you are more concerned about how you look than how your teammates fare, we beg you to turn down the opportunity to manage people. Narcissism cannot live in the soul of a manacoach.

You have to deeply care about people to be a manacoach. You have to have the courage to have tough conversations. Your teammates have to be confident that you care deeply about them, and they must unconditionally trust that you will always let them know in a timely manner where they stand, whether good or not. People want to know where they need to improve to meet the standard. The manacoach is aware of this need and addresses it on a constant basis. Study any great coach, and you'll see these traits.

Your team members need to know that you have their back. They need to know that you don't talk to others about them. They need to know that they can rely on you. If you have a problem with them as individuals, you will discuss it with them face-to-face. You put their needs in front of your own. The standards you hold them to are the ones you hold everyone to, and you don't make exceptions unless you are prepared to make the same exception for everyone under the same circumstances.

Remember that accountability and politics are inversely related, and your team members must know what they are accountable for and who they are accountable to. Decrease or confuse accountability, and you will increase the politics. Your teammates need to know that the only time you act or communicate politically is when it's for the good of the team.

It was difficult for me to learn things about myself that precluded me from being a manacoach. I'm disorganized, which makes me weak at following up. I'm self-centered, and I love being at the front of a room, messing with people's minds and leading the charge. I don't have the patience or desire to figure out if a person understands me or not. I can easily intimidate or turn people off when I'm being misinterpreted. I learned this because I had people around me who had the courage to tell me. I might not be a manacoach, but I know what one is made of. And although it's true that there are qualities that overlap, many of the qualities possessed by a leader are not pre-requisites to being a manacoach.

Manacoaches might not be leaders, but they have the magical talent, character, and ability to get things done efficiently and effectively through others.

I hope this book helps you in discovering who you are as a person, a leader, and a manacoach. I hope that *The Miracle Manager* was able to provide you with the tools to leverage your teams' talents, help you identify and fill any gaps in your abilities/approach, and get you on the path to success.

What would make me feel good about this book? If one person on this planet realized that he was a leader and made the decision to walk away from a management position. If a manager or coach was avoiding a tough conversation with someone, and after reading this book, she sat down and had a face-to-face conversation with a team member who wasn't meeting expectations. And if someone was looking to the future, knowing the current situation was wrong, he made the courageous decision to choose what was right over status or reward. A world that recognized that anyone can be a leader by simply looking to the future and doing or saying the right thing, while realizing and recognizing the unique and special talent of the manacoach . . . well, that would make me rejoice!

*Good luck with your future.*

*"Talent is God-given. Be humble. Fame is man-given.*
*Be grateful. Conceit is self-given. Be careful."*

**—JOHN WOODEN**

*a p p e n d i x*

# THE MANACOACH'S CHECKLIST

☐ 1. My own core values are in line with the core values of my company's culture.

☐ 2. If the message being communicated is criticizing, negative, judgmental, or objecting, I do it one-on-one—by phone if face-to-face is not possible, but never in writing.

☐ 3. My team knows what is expected of them, how they are being measured, and where they are not meeting critical expectations. They are given those concerns in writing only after we have had the conversation.

☐ 4. My team knows that I don't play favorites and that in the end, each of them will be held accountable in a just manner.

☐ 5. What I think, say, or do is consistent, and my team would say I walk the talk (have integrity).

☐   6.   Every waking moment, I strive to be positive, happy, and approachable.

☐   7.   I sincerely care about people and am genuinely passionate about seeing them succeed and be fulfilled.

☐   8.   Nobody approaches me with a problem without having one or more proposed solutions.

☐   9.   When I have a problem or issue with one or more team members, no matter what, I immediately meet with them and put the issue on the table.

☐   10.   When I make a mistake, I take full accountability, admit it, ask for forgiveness, and deal with any outstanding issues that I may have caused.